BAPTISTWAY AD

LARGE PRINT EDITION

Romans
A GOSPEL-CENTERED WORLDVIEW

TOM HOWE
PHIL LINEBERGER
LEIGH ANN POWERS
JESSE RINCONES

BAPTISTWAYPRESS®
Dallas, Texas

Romans: A Gospel-Centered Worldview—
BaptistWay Adult Bible Study Guide®—Large Print Edition

BAPTISTWAY PRESS® Leadership Team
Executive Director, Baptist General Convention of Texas: David Hardage
Director, Discipleship Team: Phil Miller
Publisher, BaptistWay Press®: Scott Stevens

Cover and Interior Design and Production: Desktop Miracles, Inc.
Printing: Data Reproductions Corporation

First edition: September 2015
ISBN–13: 978–1–938355–41–7

How to Make the Best Use of This Issue

Whether you're the teacher or a student—

1. Start early in the week before your class meets.

2. Overview the study. Review the table of contents and read the study introduction. Try to see how each lesson relates to the overall study.

3. Use your Bible to read and consider prayerfully the Scripture passages for the lesson. (You'll see that each writer has chosen a favorite translation for the lessons in this issue. You're free to use the Bible translation you prefer and compare it with the translation chosen for that unit, of course.)

4. After reading all the Scripture passages in your Bible, then read the writer's comments. The comments are intended to be an aid to your study of the Bible.

5. Read the small articles—"sidebars"—in each lesson. They are intended to provide additional, enrichment information and inspiration and to encourage thought and application.

6. Try to answer for yourself the questions included in each lesson. They're intended to encourage further

thought and application, and they can also be used in the class session itself.

If you're the teacher—

A. Do all of the things just mentioned, of course. As you begin the study with your class, be sure to find a way to help your class know the date on which each lesson will be studied. You might do this in one or more of the following ways:

- In the first session of the study, briefly overview the study by identifying for your class the date on which each lesson will be studied. Lead your class to write the date in the table of contents on page 11 and on the first page of each lesson.

- Make and post a chart that indicates the date on which each lesson will be studied.

- If all of your class has e-mail, send them an e-mail with the dates the lessons will be studied.

- Provide a bookmark with the lesson dates. You may want to include information about your church and then use the bookmark as an outreach tool, too. A model for a bookmark can be downloaded from www.baptistwaypress.org on the **Adults—Bible Studies** page.

- Develop a sticker with the lesson dates, and place it on the table of contents or on the back cover.

- Get a copy of the *Teaching Guide,* a companion piece to this *Study Guide.* The *Teaching Guide* contains additional Bible comments plus two teaching plans. The teaching plans in the *Teaching Guide* are intended to provide practical, easy-to-use teaching suggestions that will work in your class.

B. After you've studied the Bible passage, the lesson comments, and other material, use the teaching suggestions in the *Teaching Guide* to help you develop your plan for leading your class in studying each lesson.

C. Teaching resource items for use as handouts are available free at www.baptistwaypress.org.

D. Additional Bible study comments on the lessons are available online. Call 1–866–249–1799 or e-mail baptistway@texasbaptists.org to order the *Premium Adult Online Bible Commentary.* It is available only in electronic format (PDF) from our website, www.baptistwaypress.org. The price of these comments for the entire study is $6 for individuals and $25 for a group of five. A church or class that participates in our advance order program for free shipping can receive the *Premium Adult Online Bible Commentary* free. Call 1–866–249–1799 or see www.baptistwaypress.org to purchase or for information on participating in our free shipping program for the next study.

E. Additional teaching plans are also available in electronic format (PDF) by calling 1–866–249–1799. The price of these additional teaching plans for the entire study is $5 for an individual and $20 for a group of five. A church or class that participates in our advance order program for free shipping can receive the *Premium Adult Online Teaching Plans* free. Call 1–866–249–1799 or see www.baptistwaypress.org for information on participating in our free shipping program for the next study.

F. You also may want to get the enrichment teaching help that is provided by the *Baptist Standard* at www.baptiststandard.com. (Other class participants may find this information helpful, too.) The *Baptist Standard* is available online for an annual subscription rate of $10. Subscribe online at www.baptiststandard.com or call 214–630–4571. (A free ninety-day trial subscription is currently available.)

G. Enjoy leading your class in discovering the meaning of the Scripture passages and in applying these passages to their lives.

DO YOU USE A KINDLE?

This BaptistWay *Adult Bible Study Guide* plus *Guidance for the Seasons of Life; Living Generously for Jesus' Sake; Profiles in Character; Psalms: Songs from the Heart of Faith; Amos, Hosea, Isaiah, Micah; Jeremiah and Ezekiel; The Gospel of Matthew; The Gospel of Mark; The Gospel of Luke: Jesus' Personal Touch; The Gospel of John: Part One; The Gospel of John: Part Two; The Book of Acts: Time to Act on Acts 1:8; The Corinthian Letters: Imperatives for an Imperfect Church; Hebrews and the Letters of Peter; Letters to the Ephesians and Timothy; 14 Habits of Highly Effective Disciples; Letters to the Ephesians and Timothy; The Gospel of John; Exodus; and Created for Relationships* are now available in a Kindle edition. The easiest way to find these materials is to search for "BaptistWay" on your Kindle or go to www.amazon.com/kindle and do a search for "BaptistWay." The Kindle edition can be studied not only on a Kindle but also on a PC, Mac, iPhone, iPad, Blackberry, or Android device using the Kindle app available free from amazon.com/kindle.

AUDIO BIBLE STUDY LESSONS

Do you want to use your walk/run/ride, etc. time to study the Bible? Or maybe you're looking for a way to study the Bible when you just can't find time to read? Or maybe you know someone who has difficulty seeing to read even our *Large Print Study Guide*?

Then try our audio Bible study lessons, available on *Living Generously for Jesus' Sake*; *Profiles in Character*; *Amos, Hosea, Isaiah, Micah*; *The Gospel of Matthew*; *The Gospel of Mark*; *The Gospel of Luke*; *The Gospel of John: Part One*; *The Gospel of John: Part Two*; *The Book of Acts*; *The Corinthian Letters*; *Galatians and 1 & 2 Thessalonians*; and *The Letters of James and John*. For more information or to order, call 1–866–249–1799 or e-mail baptistway@texasbaptists.org. The files are downloaded from our website. You'll need an audio player or phone that plays MP3 files (like an iPod®, but many MP3 players are available), or you can listen on a computer.

Writers for This Study Guide

Tom Howe wrote **lessons one through four.** Tom is the senior pastor of Birdville Baptist Church, Haltom City, Texas. Dr. Howe is a graduate of East Texas Baptist University (B.S.), Beeson Divinity School at Samford University (M. Div.), and Southwestern Baptist Theological Seminary (D. Min.).

Phil Lineberger, the writer of **lessons five through seven,** served as pastor of Sugar Land Baptist Church, Sugar Land, Texas. Dr. Lineberger also served as president of the Baptist General Convention of Texas, as a trustee for William Jewell College and Dallas Baptist University, as a regent at Baylor University, and as vice-president of the Cotton Bowl Athletic Association.

Jesse Rincones wrote **lessons eight through ten.** Jesse serves as pastor of Alliance Church in Lubbock, Texas. He graduated from Texas Tech University with a B.A. in Mathematics and earned a Juris Doctor degree from the Texas Tech School of Law. Jesse serves as Executive Director of the Hispanic Baptist Convention of Texas and has served on the boards of Hereford Regional Medical Center, Pray Lubbock, Mission Lubbock, and Baptist

University of the Americas. He is married to Brenda and they share four great kids.

Leigh Ann Powers wrote **lessons eleven through thirteen.** Leigh Ann is a freelance writer and mother of three from Winters, Texas. She is a graduate of Baylor University (B.S. Ed., 1998) and Southwestern Baptist Theological Seminary (M.Div., 2004). She attends First Baptist Church in Winters, where her husband, Heath, serves as pastor. She blogs about faith, life, and family living at www.leighpowers.com.

Romans: A Gospel-Centered Worldview

Introducing

ROMANS:
A Gospel-Centered Worldview

Approaching This Study of the Book of Romans

There is an abundance of worldviews vying for people's attention and allegiance. There always has been. These include Agnosticism, Atheism, Humanism, Naturalism, Pantheism, Postmodernism, Spiritism, and Theism. Each of these views serves as the foundation of belief systems that seek to guide behaviors. One of the challenges for proponents of these various worldviews is teaching potential adherents what they should believe, why they should believe it, and how these beliefs should govern their actions.

In the Book of Romans, Paul presents a gospel-centered worldview. Paul shares the gospel (the good news of Jesus' life, death, burial, and resurrection–resulting in the opportunity for our salvation) as he explains our need, God's provision, and our response (both in conversion and beyond.) In this theological masterpiece, Paul makes a case for the claims of the gospel through a reasoned presentation of the purpose and the power of the message of Jesus Christ.

Part of Paul's reason for writing this letter to the Romans was to encourage people who were facing great persecution as a minority religion in the capital city of the Roman Empire. As part of his encouragement to his readers he writes,

> And we know that in all things God works for the good of those who love him, who have been called according to his purpose (Romans 8:28).[1]

While all things are not "good," we can trust that God is working through everything for our ultimate good and for his ultimate purpose.

He further illustrates this when he says,

> What, then, shall we say in response to this? If God is for us, who can be against us? He who did not spare his own Son–but gave him up for us all–how will he not also, along with him, graciously give us all things? (Romans 8:31–32).

One of the highlights of Romans is when Paul describes the initiative that God took in sending Jesus to provide for our greatest need, when we didn't even know the need existed:

> But God demonstrates his own love for us in this: While we were still sinners, Christ died for us (Romans 5:8).

Isn't it amazing that while we were still enemies of God, he sent his Son to be the sacrifice for our sins? This is not only a magnificent theological truth to embrace but a tremendous challenge for believers to imitate in taking the first step towards someone who needs Jesus, even if they have been our enemy. That would be true evidence of living out a gospel-centered worldview.

Since the beginning of our BaptistWay Bible study series, we have focused on the Book of Romans twice (the last time was in 2007.) Each of these studies—this one as well as the previous two—is different from the others in its approach to the individual lessons.[2]

Our fall studies focus on content from the New Testament. We believe there is tremendous value in studying the full counsel of God's word and trust that you will find this study of the Book of Romans both challenging and rewarding.

A Little Background on the Book of Romans

The Book of Romans was written by the Apostle Paul. The fact that Paul was Jewish (and a Pharisee), an apostle, a missionary, and a Roman citizen uniquely qualified him to write this deeply theological and doctrinally rich letter. Scholars believe the letter was written sometime between 54 and 58 A.D., while Paul was in Corinth. Paul wrote the letter for a number of reasons, including:

- He wanted to clarify his message and defend himself against slander that had been hurled his way.
- He desired to solidify the Romans in their faith. Because of his emphasis on salvation by faith rather than by works, some had accused him of rejecting Israel and the Jews. He wrote to reconcile the relationship between the righteousness of God and his apparent "rejection" of the Jews.
- He wanted to prepare the way for his arrival in Rome. He had long desired to visit Rome—to both encourage the church there and to use Rome as a base for the further westward expansion of the gospel to Spain. Rome was a strategic location and he could use the support of the believers there to help accomplish his mission goals.[3]

The Book of Romans addresses several themes including:

- Sin
- Salvation
- Spiritual Growth
- Sovereignty
- Service[4]

Paul addresses many theological issues in the Book of Romans, but it is more of an *occasional* theology rather than a *systematic* theology. He does not speak to eschatology, ecclesiology or delve very deeply into Christology. But he does focus a good deal on the relationship between Jews and Gentiles and the role of the Mosaic law in salvation history. As Douglas Moo states, "The first-century situation of the church at large and the church in Rome in particular leads Paul to develop his theology on certain particular issues."[5]

The Book of Romans in Our Day

How should the Book of Romans impact Jesus' followers today? As we navigate an environment that is teeming with competing worldviews, it is more valuable than ever to know what we believe and why. The Book of Romans provides a wealth of material that informs us not only of the basic facts of the gospel while also revealing the theological foundations for those facts. Its content can equip us to make a reasoned defense of our beliefs.

Another outstanding aspect of the rich treasure we have in the Book of Romans is the resource it is for sharing the gospel message with others. Many are familiar with the "Roman Road." This scriptural path (Romans 3:23, 6:23, 5:8, 10:9–10, 10:13) can be used to guide individuals to understand the gospel and to respond in faith to Jesus.

Paul's focus was on the gospel, its power, and how the worldview it provides should direct all of life. It gave him the courage to write,

> I am not ashamed of the gospel, because it is the power of God for the salvation of everyone who believes. (Romans 1:16).

ROMANS: A GOSPEL-CENTERED WORLDVIEW

Lesson 1	The Gospel is Powerful	Romans 1:1–17
Lesson 2	Exchanging God's Truth for a Lie	Romans 1:18–32
Lesson 3	Appearance vs. Obedience	Romans 2:1–29
Lesson 4	Justified by Faith	Romans 3:21–31
Lesson 5	A Faithful Example	Romans 4:1–25
Lesson 6	Rejoice in Hope	Romans 5:1–11
Lesson 7	Brought From Death to Life	Romans 6:1–23
Lesson 8	A Spirit-Controlled Life	Romans 8:1–17
Lesson 9	God Is For Us!	Romans 8:18–39

Additional Resources for Studying *Romans: A Gospel-Centered Worldview*[6]

Kenneth L. Barker and John R. Kohlenberger III. *The Expositor's Bible Commentary—Abridged Edition: New Testament.* Grand Rapids, Michigan: Zondervan, 1994.

C.K. Barrett. *Black's New Testament Commentary: The Epistle to the Romans.* Rev. ed. Peabody, Mass.: Hendrickson, 1991.

———. *A Commentary on the Epistle to the Romans.* London: Adam and Charles Black, 1957.

Karl Barth. *The Epistle to the Romans.* Translated by Edwyn C. Hoskyns. London: Humphrey Milford, 1933.

Bruce Barton, Philip Comfort, Grant Osborne, Linda K. Taylor, and Dave Veerman. *Life Application New Testament Commentary.* Carol Stream, Illinois: Tyndale House Publishers, Inc., 2001.

C.E.B. Cranfield. *A Critical and Exegetical Commentary on the Epistle to the Romans,* International Critical Commentary. 2 vols. Edinburgh: T & T Clark, 1985–1986.

J.A. Crook. *Law and Life of Rome,* 90 B.C.–A.D. 212. Ithaca, New York: Cornell University Press, 1967.

———. *Legal Advocacy in the Roman World.* London: Duckworth, 1995

A.T. Croom. *Roman Clothing and Fashion.* Charleston: Tempus, 2000.

Collin G. Kruse. *Paul's Letter to the Romans.* Pillar New Testament Commentary. Grand Rapids: William B. Eerdmans, 2012.

Douglas J. Moo. *Romans. NIV Application Commentary.* Grand Rapids: Zondervan, 2000.

Douglas J. Moo. *Romans. NICOT.* Grand Rapids: William B. Eerdmans, 1996.

Anders Nygren. *Commentary on Romans.* Translated by Carl C. Rasmussen. Philadelphia: Muhlenberg, 1949.

Peter Oakes. *Reading Romans in Pompeii: Paul's Letter at Ground Level.* Minneapolis: Fortress, 2009.

A.T. Robertson. *Word Pictures in the New Testament:* Concise Edition. Nashville, Tennessee: Holman Bible Publishers, 2000.

Charles. H. Talbert. *Romans.* Smyth & Helwys Bible Commentary. Macon: Smyth & Helwys, 2002.

Spiros Zodhiates and Warren Baker. *Hebrew-Greek Key Word Study Bible,* New International Version. Grand Rapids, Michigan: Zondervan, 1996.

NOTES ———————————————————————————————————————

1. Unless otherwise indicated, all Scripture quotations in "Introducing Romans: A Gospel-Centered Worldview" are from the New International Version (1984 edition).

2. See www.baptistwaypress.org.

3. Robert H. Mounce, *Romans,* The New American Commentary, Volume 27 (Nashville, Tennessee: B&H Publishing, 1995), 26–27.

4. Bruce Barton, Philip Comfort, Brant Osborne, Linda K. Taylor, and Dave Veerman. *Life Application New Testament Commentary* (Carol Stream, Illinois: Tyndale House Publishers, Inc., 2001), 576–578.

5. Douglas J. Moo, "Romans" *The NIV Application Commentary* (Grand Rapids: Zondervan, 2000), 20.

6. Listing a book does not imply full agreement by the writers or BAPTISTWAY PRESS® with all of its comments.

FOCAL TEXT
Romans 1:1–17

BACKGROUND
Romans 1:1–17

LESSON 1

The Gospel is Powerful

MAIN IDEA

The gospel is the power of God for the salvation of everyone who believes.

QUESTION TO EXPLORE

How has the power of the gospel been revealed?

STUDY AIM

To comprehend the revelation of the gospel and its power

QUICK READ

Like Paul, we should not be ashamed of the gospel, for it contains the power of God for the salvation our world so desperately needs.

Introduction

When I was eleven, I lived in a town of 200 people, three stores, and only one major business: an electric cooperative that supplied power to the entire region. Often high winds or wintry weather would knock down some of the power lines, causing large parts of the region to lose electricity. Our house was next door to the power station, though, so we always had electricity no matter how many lines were down. The lines from the station to our house were a conduit of constant power. Likewise, the gospel itself is the power of God for the salvation of everyone who believes. God saves through the good news of Jesus' life, death, and resurrection.[1]

ROMANS 1:1–17

[1] Paul, a servant of Christ Jesus, called to be an apostle and set apart for the gospel of God—[2] the gospel he promised beforehand through his prophets in the Holy Scriptures [3] regarding his Son, who as to his human nature was a descendant of David, [4] and who through the Spirit of holiness was declared with power to be the Son of God by his resurrection from the dead: Jesus Christ our Lord. [5] Through him and for his name's sake, we received grace and apostleship to call people from among all the Gentiles to the obedience that comes from faith. [6] And you also

are among those who are called to belong to Jesus Christ. [7] To all in Rome who are loved by God and called to be saints: Grace and peace to you from God our Father and from the Lord Jesus Christ.

[8] First, I thank my God through Jesus Christ for all of you, because your faith is being reported all over the world. [9] God, whom I serve with my whole heart in preaching the gospel of his Son, is my witness how constantly I remember you [10] in my prayers at all times; and I pray that now at last by God's will the way may be opened for me to come to you.

[11] I long to see you so that I may impart to you some spiritual gift to make you strong— [12] that is, that you and I may be mutually encouraged by each other's faith. [13] I do not want you to be unaware, brothers, that I planned many times to come to you (but have been prevented from doing so until now) in order that I might have a harvest among you, just as I have had among the other Gentiles.

[14] I am obligated both to Greeks and non-Greeks, both to the wise and the foolish. [15] That is why I am so eager to preach the gospel also to you who are at Rome.

[16] I am not ashamed of the gospel, because it is the power of God for the salvation of everyone who believes: first for the Jew, then for the Gentile. [17] For in the gospel a righteousness from God is revealed, a righteousness that is by faith from first to last, just as it is written: "The righteous will live by faith."

The Gospel's Powerful Call (1:1–7)

Paul introduced himself by a powerful, threefold calling on his life: 1) to be a slave to Jesus; 2) to be an apostle; and 3) to proclaim the gospel of God. The letter begins *Paulos doulos,* which means "Paul slave." *Doulos* is sometimes translated as "bondservant" or "servant," but most scholars think he meant "slave." The first part of the call in his life was to be a slave to Christ. Jesus was his master, not just his teacher, guide, or friend. The tagline of Paul's life was "slave of Christ." His calling was based on his understanding of Jesus' authority and lordship in his life.

Another aspect of Paul's calling was to be an apostle of Jesus Christ. Paul came out of a life that was antagonistic to the gospel and into a life of preaching it. Seventeen years had passed from Paul's conversion to his first missionary journey, on which he served alongside Barnabas (Galatians 1:13–2:1). Paul's life is a reminder that sometimes God takes time to prepare us for the task he has for us. Moses wandered privately in the wilderness for forty years before he led the people of Israel out of Egypt and back into that same wilderness for another forty years. David became king about thirteen years after Samuel anointed him. Though God still calls us to specific offices today (preacher, teacher, evangelist, deacon, etc.), we often need a time of preparation for these roles.

Lastly, Paul was called to fulfill a unique and special purpose. God did not call him to help society or benefit people (although he did both), but to preach the gospel. The gospel is the good news that Jesus Christ left heaven to come to earth, lived a sinless life, died for our sins, rose again, ascended back to his throne in heaven, and now waits to return to the earth for his people.

Jesus came to address humanity's sin and impending judgment. He came to give us abundant life, joy, and peace. Christ's message is the message of hope and reconciliation. Paul's task was to share that message. His calling was so great that he gave his entire life to it. God had done a miraculous work in his life and he was completely committed to God's purpose for him.

Likewise, God has a calling on our lives as well, in one of three ways: general, specific, or vocational. First, God calls on all people to accept his gospel message, and upon receiving Christ, to walk in obedience to him (Romans 1:5), to belong to Christ (1:6) and to be saints, that is to be sanctified (1:7). Additionally, all Christians also have a specific calling in their lives related to a spiritual gift, talent, role, or task (12:3–8). Finally, some people have been called to serve God as their vocation (career), including preachers, ministers, missionaries, professors, and other careers of Christian service (1 Corinthians 12:12–28; Ephesians 4:11–16).

The Gospel's Powerful Motivation (1:8–15)

The gospel motivated Paul in four ways. Paul's first motivation for preaching the gospel was the people who needed to hear it. For example, he was motivated by the reputation of the Romans whose faith was being reported all over the world (1:8); he wrote about his desire to see them (1:13). Even in his absence, Paul devoted himself to pray for the Romans (1:10). Though Paul's passion in this text referred to the Roman people specifically, his passion extended to all people so that they would be saved. The need for others to hear God's message of salvation should motivate us as well.

Another motivation for Paul was his love for God. Paul had experienced an incredible outpouring of God's mercy and grace despite his sin. In turn, Paul's love for God became the motivation that compelled him to serve Jesus. With all that God has done for each of us, we should also be driven to serve him. He has loved us, forgiven us, and blessed us greatly. We should express the same devotion as Paul by serving God in any way he may call us.

A third motivation for Paul was to see changed lives. He knew God's message and gifts would change the lives of the Romans by giving them strength (1:11). Strength can be measured in different ways. Some need strength to endure difficulties, trials, or persecution. Paul would eventually meet the Romans face-to-face and experience martyrdom for the sake of the gospel. He would embody for them the very strength he wanted to give to them. Strength also means to be bold in faith, rich in love and kindness, and steadfast in the face of temptation.

Changed lives become encouraged lives (1:12). The encouragement that the gospel gives us is not a simple wish for a happy life, but instead is fueled by eternal hope that changes our worldview. There are two meaning of hope: 1) We might get lucky and something good may happen to us; or 2) A certainty that we will experience something for our good. Because of all that Christ has done and has promised, believers have certainty that God will do something good for us in the future. Our hope is focused on the future, not our present circumstances.

Finally, Paul was motivated out of obligation (1:14), which was not a somber task of drudgery, but a call that Paul eagerly accepted (1:15). He was obliged to serve Jews and Gentiles, wise and foolish, and everyone else because of his love for God, his love for others, his experience of salvation, and his witness to the practical power of the gospel.

The Gospel's Power for Salvation (1:16–17)

Paul was setting up the rest of his letter in Romans 1:16–17. The gospel message to which Paul was called is the hope for all humanity. Paul knew this because he had both seen and experienced this hope for himself. He experienced it in his conversion and then he had seen hope arise in countless others who had given their lives to God through faith in Jesus Christ. Paul had endured incredible difficulties for the sake of the gospel (see 2 Corinthians 6:4–5, 11:23–33), yet he confidently said, "I am not ashamed of the gospel" (Rom. 1:16). His life demonstrated his belief in the power of the gospel to change people and sustain them in times of hardship.

Paul listed the two powerful effects that the gospel brings: salvation and righteousness. The initial act of the gospel is to bring redemption from sin, its immediate control, and its eternal consequences. Throughout the rest of his letter to the Romans, Paul laid out the damage sin causes and the judgment that follows. Jesus' sacrificial death satisfies the need for judgment. Christ also empowers us to be transformed (12:1–2) so that sin does not control us. However, the ultimate form of salvation is the freedom from death and eternal separation from God (5:1).

Salvation is available to all because all people need it. Even though salvation is available to all, not everyone will receive it. It is free but not automatic. It is only effective for those who believe. Paul added that stipulation as the step of faith every person must choose to take. We must believe (trust in the work of Christ) in order to participate in God's salvation (10:9–10).

The second effect of the gospel is righteousness. Our efforts to become righteous are not sufficient. Isaiah 64:6

declares that human-based righteousness is like filthy rags. This is a hard thing for some people to hear. We like to think we are acceptable or good enough. We are irritated at the notion that we have shortcomings; we don't like our actions to be judged. However, our sin taints us so that we cannot enter the presence of a holy God, no matter how much we try to clean ourselves.

Romans 3 describes how all people fall short of God's glory and his expectation of righteousness. But God loves us so much that he still made a way for us to enter his presence (5:8). He saves us and makes us righteous so that we can remain in his presence. In this new righteousness, we are no longer living life under our own inadequate power, but through the power of God's Holy Spirit in us (Romans 8). Just as we received salvation by our belief, we also receive our new righteousness by faith. We cannot achieve righteousness ourselves, but we can take hold of what God has given to us by faith.

Implications and Actions

God has demonstrated his power and his love in the gospel message. Our sin has led us away from God. We are powerless to reach him by ourselves. The gospel explains how God remedied our situation. Jesus was God. He became human. He lived a righteous (perfect) life. He died as the sacrificial substitute for all who would believe and receive his salvation by faith. He also extended his righteousness to us. Have you received salvation by faith in Jesus? Do you trust God by faith to make you righteous? If you have experienced the power of the gospel, how can you help others to do the same?

CALLING

Calling (being called) in the Bible has three components. It begins with a divine summoning, similar to a father calling to a child, "Son, get in here now!" which sounds quite different from, "Son, could you come over here when you get a chance?" The former is the calling that God has on his people. We can choose to reject God's voice, but we are in immediate disobedience when we do.

The second part of a biblical calling is the effectual process of being prepared by God for a purpose or task. Much like Moses or Paul were prepared for their tasks, God does not summon us to do anything without giving us the talent, training, and skills to complete the task. The final part of God's calling is the commissioning, or being sent out. It may be soon after his summoning, or there may be a period of growing in faith and character to prepare us for the task ahead.

APOSTLE

Apostolos means, "messenger." The word can be used in two ways. In one sense, it means someone who carries a message. In the religious meaning, the term is the functionary title of one of the early Christian leaders who had seen Jesus in person and who were called to the initial task of advancing the gospel. This meaning is usually designated by the first letter of the word being capitalized, similar to titles like Ambassador, Governor, or Senator.

Peter, John, and the rest of the disciples were Apostles because they walked with Jesus. Paul attained his apostleship on the road to Damascus as "one abnormally born" (1 Corinthians 15:8). Although we can be messengers of the gospel and thereby be called apostles (little "a"), the title Apostle (capital "A") is reserved for those early Christian leaders. Successive generations of Christians did not take the title for themselves.

QUESTIONS

1. Compare being a "servant of Christ" to being a "slave of Christ." What does it mean to you that Paul called himself a "slave of Christ?"

2. Remembering that apostle means "messenger," how can we be "apostles" today?

3. Do you feel God has called you to do something specific for him? Explain.

4. What motivates you to share the gospel? How do your motivations compare with Paul's?

5. What is the difference between the gospel bringing us salvation and it bringing us righteousness?

NOTES ───────────────────────────────

1. Unless otherwise indicated, all Scripture quotations in lessons 1–13 are from the New International Version (1984 edition).

LESSON 2

Exchanging God's Truth for a Lie

MAIN IDEA

Ignoring God allows sin to flourish.

QUESTION TO EXPLORE

What are the causes and results of ignoring God?

STUDY AIM

To identify the causes and results of ignoring God

QUICK READ

Sin flourishes when we live life without God. God will allow us to ignore him, but we must live with the natural consequences.

Introduction

Why does God allow sin to flourish? Will the world continue to get worse? In our ever-changing culture, is sin still sin? At times, it seems that there is no consequence for living as though God does not exist. People continue to sin without any reservation and the world continues its downhill slide. The focal passage of this lesson, Romans 1:18–32, speaks to this issue. It lays out both the cause and the effect of ignoring God, as well as his wrath for sin that is certain.

ROMANS 1:18–32

18 The wrath of God is being revealed from heaven against all the godlessness and wickedness of men who suppress the truth by their wickedness, 19 since what may be known about God is plain to them, because God has made it plain to them. 20 For since the creation of the world God's invisible qualities—his eternal power and divine nature—have been clearly seen, being understood from what has been made, so that men are without excuse.

21 For although they knew God, they neither glorified him as God nor gave thanks to him, but their thinking became futile and their foolish hearts were darkened. 22 Although they claimed to be wise, they became fools

²³ and exchanged the glory of the immortal God for images made to look like mortal man and birds and animals and reptiles.

²⁴ Therefore God gave them over in the sinful desires of their hearts to sexual impurity for the degrading of their bodies with one another. ²⁵ They exchanged the truth of God for a lie, and worshiped and served created things rather than the Creator—who is forever praised. Amen.

²⁶ Because of this, God gave them over to shameful lusts. Even their women exchanged natural relations for unnatural ones. ²⁷ In the same way the men also abandoned natural relations with women and were inflamed with lust for one another. Men committed indecent acts with other men, and received in themselves the due penalty for their perversion.

²⁸ Furthermore, since they did not think it worthwhile to retain the knowledge of God, he gave them over to a depraved mind, to do what ought not to be done. ²⁹ They have become filled with every kind of wickedness, evil, greed and depravity. They are full of envy, murder, strife, deceit and malice. They are gossips, ³⁰ slanderers, God-haters, insolent, arrogant and boastful; they invent ways of doing evil; they disobey their parents; ³¹ they are senseless, faithless, heartless, ruthless. ³² Although they know God's righteous decree that those who do such things deserve death, they not only continue to do these very things but also approve of those who practice them.

The Wrath of God (1:18)

The wrath of God is not a popular theme. Romans 1:18 follows two verses that speak of being unashamed of the gospel. God's wrath is a part of his gospel message. He will deal with those who choose to disobey him. The wrath of God is not to be confused with human anger. The latter is an uncontrolled, irrational emotion often wrapped in jealousy, vanity, malice, revenge, or selfishness. On the contrary, the wrath of God is based on his just nature. It is a correct and right response to sin. A holy God cannot condone or make light of sin. If God allowed sin and evil to run amuck without consequence, then he would not be a just God. God's compassion and righteousness are two aspects of his nature that are revealed as love and wrath respectively. His holiness will not entertain sin, so consequentially, sin separates the sinner from God.

Six Causes of Ignoring God (1:18–24)

This passage outlines in great detail six causes or reasons people ignore God and his standard of holiness and righteousness. While Paul must have had his own culture in mind when he wrote this letter to the Roman people, these six causes characterize today's culture as well.

Wickedness (1:18). The entire focal text of this lesson describes a downward spiral of suppressing truth, wallowing in sin, moving away from truth, deeper involvement in sin, and so on. Wickedness draws people away from God, while walking with God draws people away from wickedness.

Not glorifying God (1:21). The first question of the Westminster Confession is, "What is the chief end of man?" The answer is, "Man's chief end is to glorify God and to enjoy him forever." This doctrine is based on 1 Peter 4:11, 1 Corinthians 10:31, and other verses. Once someone forfeits glorifying God, then ignoring him altogether is a natural consequence. Moses longed to see God's glory (Exodus 33:18) and Jesus said that glory was the bond between the Father and Son and was extended to all Christians (John 17:20–23).

No gratitude for God (1:21). A lack of gratitude reveals a heart of independent selfishness, or at least self-centeredness. We as humans tend to not be thankful for the things we earn or think we deserve. We forget God's great provision in our lives, from the breaths that we take every moment of every day to the talents he has given us. We depend on our abilities, ambition, and intelligence, and we lose dependence on God except in the worst of situations. Our lack of gratefulness leads to diminishing devotion to God and to ignoring him more and more until we don't even think of him at all.

Futile minds (1:21–22). The refusal to acknowledge God leads people to focus on the here and now instead of focusing on God and important and eternal things. The word "amuse" is a combination of "muse" with the prefix "a", which is a prefix that negates the word it is attached to. "Muse" means to think about something. To negate that means not thinking about something. Although amusement means to be entertained, it also has the underlying idea of turning the brain off. This results in a lack of critical thinking, analysis, and contemplation. The more we entertain ourselves with mindless and useless pursuits, the more futile our thinking becomes, and the more we ignore God.

Seeking glory in things (1:23). If glorifying God is the chief end of humanity, then doing anything less leaves a void in one's heart that needs to be filled. "Things" become the object of our wonder and admiration. We can glory in the beauty of the mountains, the power of a waterfall, the children we have raised, the success we have achieved, or the accumulation of possessions and wealth. We can find endless substitutes for the focus we should place on God; the more we indulge in these inferior substitutes, the more we ignore him.

Worshipping creation (1:23–24). Another expression of ignoring God is worshipping created things. Sometimes our Father in heaven can be replaced by Mother Nature; our Master can be replaced with MasterCard®. What people worship can be identified by: 1) what they spend money on; 2) what they think about; and 3) what they talk about. Anything can occupy the mind, heart, and mouth as a substitute for worshipping God—wealth, sex, power, work, recreation, etc. When we worship these things, we are distracted from worshipping the Creator of them.

The Results of Ignoring God (1:24–31)

Verse 24 begins with the word "therefore," a word that could equal a pronouncement of judgment. Because humanity has walked away from God, it will experience the consequences of its rebellious actions. Paul offered a long list of results that can be summarized by three generalities, twenty-three specific vices, and one final judgment. Although the list Paul wrote is not exhaustive (there are other sins not found in this list), it does represent the entire spectrum of a life apart from God.

God's judgment can be active or passive. For the most part, Romans 1 reveals God's passive judgment. Ignoring God opens the door to evil in our lives. His passive judgment allows us to continue to live without him and thus receive all the natural consequences of such a life. For example, a person who drinks without restraint will experience health problems. If you gossip, people won't trust you. This is passive judgment.

Paul summarized three passive consequences of God's wrath by using the phrase "God gave them over." God gave sinful people over to the sinful desires of the heart (1:24); he gave them over to degrading their bodies with shameful lusts (1:24, 26); he gave them over to think with

a depraved mind (1:28). These three describe the total-
ity of a person: emotion, will, flesh, and intellect. Once
someone ignores God, the natural consequences affect
the entire person.

Verses 24–31 list twenty-three specific sins that result
from ignoring God. Two sins of the flesh are listed: sexual
immorality and homosexuality (1:24–27). Neither of these
sins carries the stigma that they once did in our culture,
and anyone who opposes sexual freedom is labeled as an
intolerant prude. Nevertheless, the Bible says that these
two actions demonstrate God's passive judgment. God
allows people to have what they want, which is freedom
from his rules. Unfortunately, living apart from God's
guidelines and authority will result in natural, negative
consequences. Talk with anyone who has had an affair,
and they will tell you the price paid for infidelity.

Paul then listed four all-consuming general sins:
wickedness, evil, greed, and depravity (1:29). These sins
consume a person's heart and mind. They are not just
one-time acts; they can become a habitual lifestyle. People
who can be described in these terms are far from God and
have been for a long time. They will most likely admit that
they have no desire for God, either denying his existence
altogether or not caring if he exists or not. They are likely
dismissive of God and may be antagonistic to religion or
religious people.

The next seven consequential sins all deal with broken
human relationships: envy, murder, strife, deceit, malice,

gossip, and slander (1:29–30). Ignoring God leads to self-ishness (or at least self-centeredness), which leads people away from thinking of others, and results in damaged relationships. A life without God devolves into a "survival of the fittest" mentality that rewards strife, deceit, and malice over sacrifice and service. God has a greater calling on our lives. We are to serve one another and treat others with his love. John wrote that loving others shows that we know God (1 John 3:14–16).

The next four sins are the result of pride: God-haters, insolent, arrogant, and boastful (1:30). God-haters include anyone who refuses to recognize an outside authority figure. They have no need for God in their lives. They are so selfish that they do not have time for God or others. Plus, they want everyone else to love and admire them as much as they love and admire themselves. They are boastful, conceited, and draw attention to themselves. On the contrary, someone who loves God would seek to point others to God, not to themself. Those who live in pride seek to benefit themselves, while the godly want to draw attention to the Lord.

In verse 30, Paul listed two more results of ignoring God: inventing evil and disobeying parents (1:30). The characteristic of inventing evil summarizes the entire list of disobedient acts and takes it to its logical end. For some people, their proud self-absorption, mixed with a predisposition toward sin, leads them to find new and innovative ways to sin, pushing the boundaries of right and wrong.

This total disregard for God's law is accentuated by a person's disobedience to parents. This demonstrates a lack of respect for all authority and boundaries, both of which have been set in place by God for a person's protection and provision.

Finally, Paul listed four sins of negation: people who are senseless, faithless, heartless, and ruthless (1:31). These words describe a person void of anything good or constructive. They describe the sins in our world (or the people who commit them) that are without thoughtfulness, honor, love, compassion, kindness, or pity. These actions demonstrate how someone could act without any remorse or conscience. Unfortunately, a cursory glance online would provide ample examples of such senseless behavior, which is the logical end of rejecting God, the source of goodness.

The ultimate result of ignoring God is death (1:32). All people will give an account to God one day (14:12). Rejecting God leads to three consequences: 1) eternal death, or separation from God forever; 2) spiritual deadness that can be experienced in part in this life; 3) the need for the vicarious death of Jesus on the cross to redeem those who have sinned.

Implications and Actions

Most people do not ignore God with intention or malice in their hearts. Rather, ignoring God results from neglect.

We get busy with our rushed lives and fail to think about him or to spend time with him. When we neglect him, our affection for him slowly fades. We allow our minds and actions to wander away from God, and soon we are serving the creation rather than the Creator. God's passive wrath will leave us to live in our sinful natures, and we will slip further and further away from him. All along, we know we are not where we need to be, yet we involve ourselves in the things we know we should avoid. Hopefully, we will come to the point of recognizing our need to turn back to God. God does not desire this rebellious path for us, but he will allow it—as well as the consequences that result. Let us instead choose to worship and adore him.

GENERAL REVELATION

General revelation refers to how God has revealed himself to humanity in a general sense. God has revealed himself to us through creation, history, and humanity. He reveals himself through creation (nature) by the intricacies, patterns, and brilliance of creation, as well as our ability to understand them. His hand has been seen through history in a large scale way (the miraculous evacuation of Dunkirk, for example) and in a much more personal, individual way.

Humanity reveals God through our complex physical structure and mental capacities, along with our internal qualities of morality and spirituality. We make moral judgments beyond ourselves, without considering our likes or dislikes, even if something is not beneficial to us. We are spiritual beings, above and beyond our physical bodies, which points to God.

General revelation is not intended to prove God's existence. Paul was not trying to do so in Romans 1. He was establishing the principle that humans have a higher responsibility than to live strictly for themselves and the moment in which they live, and that they know this truth innately.

DANGERS OF IGNORING GOD

Which of these six causes of ignoring God is your greatest temptation?

- Wickedness (willful ongoing involvement with sin)
- Failure to give God glory
- Failure to give God thanks
- Purposeless, mindless living
- Seeking glory in things (possessions)
- Worshipping creation

What steps will you take to address these temptations?

QUESTIONS

1. Discuss how Romans 1 describes the wrath of God as "passive judgment" compared to God's "active judgment."

2. What do you think about God's passive judgment, that is, his giving us over to our sins? Talk about what it means to be given over to the lusts of the heart or the depravity of the mind.

3. How have you experienced a downward cycle of ignoring God? What caused you to make a change?

4. Have you seen the consequences of ignoring God played out in someone's life? In your own life? What did you see?

LESSON 3

Appearance vs. Obedience

MAIN IDEA

The remedy for judgment is obedience, not religious heritage.

QUESTION TO EXPLORE

Do we trust our religious heritage to save us from God's judgment?

STUDY AIM

To become convinced that my obedience to God (not my religious heritage) is the remedy for his righteous judgment

QUICK READ

God cares more about our obedience to him than how we present ourselves outwardly.

Introduction

Some of Paul's Roman readers were Jewish and would have applauded wholeheartedly his statements in the first chapter. However, his tonal change in the second chapter would have quickly deflated their enthusiasm. Paul explained that the Gentiles would be judged for ignoring God (1:18–32), but the Jews would also be judged. Neither their religious heritage nor their personal self-righteousness would spare them from God's judgment. When God chose David to be king, he said to Samuel, "The LORD does not look at the things man looks at. Man looks at the outward appearance, but the Lord looks at the heart" (1 Samuel 16:7). God is more interested in a person's heart, not just an outward appearance of righteousness without any real spiritual substance (Romans 2:29).

ROMANS 2

¹ You, therefore, have no excuse, you who pass judgment on someone else, for at whatever point you judge the other, you are condemning yourself, because you who pass judgment do the same things. ² Now we know that God's judgment against those who do such things is based on truth. ³ So when you, a mere man, pass judgment on them and yet do the same things, do you think you will escape God's judgment? ⁴ Or do you

show contempt for the riches of his kindness, tolerance and patience, not realizing that God's kindness leads you toward repentance?

5 But because of your stubbornness and your unrepentant heart, you are storing up wrath against yourself for the day of God's wrath, when his righteous judgment will be revealed. 6 God "will give to each person according to what he has done." 7 To those who by persistence in doing good seek glory, honor and immortality, he will give eternal life. 8 But for those who are self-seeking and who reject the truth and follow evil, there will be wrath and anger. 9 There will be trouble and distress for every human being who does evil: first for the Jew, then for the Gentile; 10 but glory, honor and peace for everyone who does good: first for the Jew, then for the Gentile. 11 For God does not show favoritism.

12 All who sin apart from the law will also perish apart from the law, and all who sin under the law will be judged by the law. 13 For it is not those who hear the law who are righteous in God's sight, but it is those who obey the law who will be declared righteous. 14 (Indeed, when Gentiles, who do not have the law, do by nature things required by the law, they are a law for themselves, even though they do not have the law, 15 since they show that the requirements of the law are written on their hearts, their consciences also bearing witness, and their thoughts now accusing, now even defending them.) 16 This will take place on the day when God will

judge men's secrets through Jesus Christ, as my gospel declares.

17 Now you, if you call yourself a Jew; if you rely on the law and brag about your relationship to God; 18 if you know his will and approve of what is superior because you are instructed by the law; 19 if you are convinced that you are a guide for the blind, a light for those who are in the dark, 20 an instructor of the foolish, a teacher of infants, because you have in the law the embodiment of knowledge and truth— 21 you, then, who teach others, do you not teach yourself? You who preach against stealing, do you steal? 22 You who say that people should not commit adultery, do you commit adultery? You who abhor idols, do you rob temples? 23 You who brag about the law, do you dishonor God by breaking the law? 24 As it is written: "God's name is blasphemed among the Gentiles because of you."

25 Circumcision has value if you observe the law, but if you break the law, you have become as though you had not been circumcised. 26 If those who are not circumcised keep the law's requirements, will they not be regarded as though they were circumcised? 27 The one who is not circumcised physically and yet obeys the law will condemn you who, even though you have the written code and circumcision, are a lawbreaker.

28 A man is not a Jew if he is only one outwardly, nor is circumcision merely outward and physical. 29 No, a man is a Jew if he is one inwardly; and circumcision

is circumcision of the heart, by the Spirit, not by the written code. Such a man's praise is not from men, but from God.

Appearance: How to be a Hypocrite (2:1–11)

These verses identify characteristics of a hypocrite. First, hypocrites pass judgment on others while doing the very same things themselves (2:1). It is easy to think of people who commit the sins listed in Romans 1, but it is more challenging to examine our hearts honestly and admit our own sin. We have plenty of excuses for our behavior. We bristle at what others have done to us, but we justify our own shortcomings. David was quick to condemn the sheep-stealer of Nathan's story, but never considered his own actions until their ugliness was presented to him (2 Samuel 12). Although we may not be guilty of *all* of the sins mentioned in Romans 1, we nevertheless have sinned and are not worthy to judge anyone else.

A hypocrite also expects partiality from God (Rom. 2:2–3). Jesus' parable of the unforgiving servant (Matthew 18:21–35) tells about a man who is forgiven a great debt he owed but then demands payment for a small debt owed to him. Likewise, we want forgiveness from God when we sin, but then we treat others with contempt for lesser sins. We want mercy for ourselves but expect

God to mete out justice to others, especially when they have wronged us. Though we may want preferential treatment, God does not play favorites.

Hypocrites place importance on their own self-righteousness (Rom. 2:4–7). For example, we take for granted God's grace and remain stubborn and unrepentant. We refuse to admit that our hearts need to be cleaned. Self-righteous people overlook, minimize, and forget about God's kindness, tolerance, and patience. God does not demonstrate his mercy just to make us feel better, but rather to lead us to repentance and obedience. Hypocrites play their "get-out-of-jail-free" card without demonstrating any real remorse. It is very difficult for self-righteous people to repent (Deuteronomy 10:16; Jeremiah 4:4). However, one day all people will be recognized for their faithfulness to God or for their stubborn unrepentance (Rom. 14:12; 1 Corinthians 3:10–15; 2 Corinthians 5:10; Matthew 24—25).

In addition, hypocrites are self-seeking, reject truth, and revel in evil (Rom. 2:8–11). Keep in mind that in this passage, Paul was not referring to the unbelieving Gentiles, but to the self-righteous Jews. Selfishness is an antonym for love. Love focuses on the needs of others while selfishness focuses inwardly on one's own needs. God will reward those who seek him and who love others, but those who seek self and evil will experience his wrath.

Judgment for a Lack of Obedience (2:12–24)

God is less interested in our play-acting abilities and is more interested in our owning a sincere faith that is focused on him. Having the law is not good enough. Knowing the law is not enough. Those who *obey* the law will be declared righteous (2:13), but only Jesus was able to do that. Jesus set the standard of perfect obedience to the law. For those who have the law, judgment will come based on the law. Those who are unaware of it are judged apart from the law. This seems harsh, but Paul was building his case for Romans 3:10 (no one is righteous) and Romans 3:23 (for all have sinned) and Romans 3:24 (all can be justified through Christ alone).

All disobedience against God will be judged. Those who are aware of the law will be condemned under it because they did not keep it; however, this does not mean that those who were unaware of the law are free from judgment. The Gentiles are also held accountable for their sins because of their moral awareness through their conscience (2:15). They knew inwardly the difference between right and wrong even though they did not have the law.

Regardless of our background (religious or not), all of us will be held accountable to God for the lives we live. There will be no excuse. Each person's conscience communicates right versus wrong. Romans 2:15 declares that every person—Jew and Gentile—innately knows the requirements of God's law. Their conscience bears witness and their thoughts condemn (or acquit) them. Because no one keeps the law completely at all times, all people are guilty of sin.

The Jews had reason to brag. They were the chosen people of God, possessing the law and having a relationship with God. They could brag about knowing God's will and experiencing a superior way of life. However, they could not brag about keeping the law. They, too, fell short (Rom. 2:23).

Romans 2:21–33 lists several ways people demonstrate hypocrisy: teaching others without being teachable; preaching about stealing but being a thief; condemning adultery in others but practicing adultery; and condemning idolatry but stealing from temples. For all their privilege and blessings, the Jews failed in the same ways as the Gentiles. Likewise, we fail in these same ways. For this reason, we too deserve judgment for our disobedience, just like the Gentiles and Jews of ancient times.

Obedience and Genuine Faith (2:25–29)

Paul used the term "circumcision" to represent those who had been given the law. For the Jews, circumcision was the outward expression of obedience to, and identification with, God. The act itself held no value if the person's heart was defiant against God; such obedience to the law was useless without a submissive heart. Genuine faith is demonstrated by genuine, heart-oriented faithfulness. Obedience to God's law—whether the law given to Moses or the law written on the heart of all people—trumps external appearances.

In an unexpected twist, Paul said that those who walk in obedience and who have a correct "law of the heart" (not just an outward symbol) will condemn those who keep up an appearance but fail to walk in obedience. To a Jew, being judged by a Gentile was the ultimate sacrilege and scandal.

Obedience and genuine faith are the true evidences of belonging to God. Paul even redefined what it meant to be a Jew (2:28–29). The written code had less to do with being a Jew than the attitude of one's heart. Paul explained that "circumcision of the heart" performed by the Spirit is what truly makes someone God's child. He was driving home the point that religious heritage, customs, and practices do not matter before God. Those things may impress others, but not God. God does not show favoritism, but receives all who seek him—regardless of their spiritual heritage.

Implications and Actions

While Jewish heritage, customs, and habits would not be an issue in the church today, we as believers certainly develop our own systems by which we judge others and ourselves. We may base our righteousness on what we give, how we serve, how often we attend church, or what we abstain from doing (drinking, playing the lottery, committing adultery, etc.). Like the Jewish practices of Paul's day, obedience to God is a way to express our love toward God, but we must not allow such obedience to become the sole measure of our standing before God.

In this early portion of Romans, Paul was laying the foundation for the need of justification by Christ. However, these verses warn us that even after we have received salvation, we must not fall into the trap of judging ourselves or others based on outward appearances. God cares about what's going on in the heart. He wants our obedience to be motivated by a heart of gratitude for the love he has shown us through Christ.

HYPOCRITE

In the movie *The Mask*, Stanley Ipkis is the timid, mild-mannered banker who is pushed around and disregarded until he discovers a mask with extraordinary powers. With it, he becomes powerful, outgoing, and flamboyant. Removing the mask causes him to return to his former self.

This movie illustrates the classic definition of hypocrisy.

The Greek word *hypokrites* refers to a masked actor on the stage in a theater. The English derivative keeps a similar spelling and meaning. To be a hypocrite is to wear a mask and play a part in front of people, but to be someone else altogether underneath the veneer. Certainly, many genuine people live and work in all spheres of life, but unfortunately, many people simply wear a mask, metaphorically speaking. God desires his followers to be authentic in their relationships, including their relationship with him.

HOW NOT TO BE A HYPOCRITE

Here are some practical ways to avoid being a hypocrite:

- Love others unconditionally and leave judgment to God.

- Walk in obedience to God, one decision at a time.

- Focus on and appreciate God's grace every day.

- Understand that God is impartial toward all people.

- Be teachable.

- Repent of sin as soon as the Holy Spirit convicts you.

- Seek the Kingdom of God continuously.

- Learn and live in God's truth; avoid the lies and deception of the world.

QUESTIONS

1. If Christians were honest, we would admit that
    we are judgmental toward others even though we
    continue to wrestle with sin. What is the cure for
    such hypocrisy?

2. Romans 2:5 says we store up wrath for the day of
    God's judgment. Does this apply to Christians?
    Explain.

3. How do Christians show favoritism today? How does your church show favoritism? How might your class show favoritism?

4. Explain in your own words the difference between "outward circumcision" and the "circumcision of the heart."

5. Can a person live in self-condemnation even though Christ has already forgiven him or her? How can a person find freedom from self-condemnation?

FOCAL TEXT

Romans 3:21–31

BACKGROUND

Romans 3:21–31

LESSON 4

Justified by Faith

MAIN IDEA

We are made right with God
by faith in Jesus Christ.

QUESTION TO EXPLORE

What do we trust in to make
us right with God?

STUDY AIM

To resolve that faith alone makes
me right with God and to place
my total trust in Christ

QUICK READ

Jesus is the revealed righteousness
of God who leads us to experience
his righteousness by faith.

Introduction

Romans 3:21–31 details God's plan of dealing with our unrighteousness. Chapters 1 and 2 of the Book of Romans lead up to this point. The Gentiles are not righteous because of their sin apart from the law. The Jews are not righteous because of their sin under the law. The verdict is clear: no one is righteous (Romans 3:10–12). We are not righteous on our own, and we cannot achieve righteousness. (See the sidebar regarding righteousness). We cannot earn righteousness, but we can receive it by faith in Jesus Christ.

ROMANS 3:21–31

21 But now a righteousness from God, apart from law, has been made known, to which the Law and the Prophets testify. 22 This righteousness from God comes through faith in Jesus Christ to all who believe. There is no difference, 23 for all have sinned and fall short of the glory of God, 24 and are justified freely by his grace through the redemption that came by Christ Jesus. 25 God presented him as a sacrifice of atonement, through faith in his blood. He did this to demonstrate his justice, because in his forbearance he had left the sins committed beforehand unpunished—26 he did it to demonstrate his justice at the present time, so as to be

just and the one who justifies those who have faith in Jesus.

27 Where, then, is boasting? It is excluded. On what principle? On that of observing the law? No, but on that of faith. 28 For we maintain that a man is justified by faith apart from observing the law. 29 Is God the God of Jews only? Is he not the God of Gentiles too? Yes, of Gentiles too, 30 since there is only one God, who will justify the circumcised by faith and the uncircumcised through that same faith. 31 Do we, then, nullify the law by this faith? Not at all! Rather, we uphold the law.

A Righteousness from God is Revealed (3:21–22a)

God revealed his righteousness according to his timing (see also 1:17; 3:19, and Galatians 4:4–5). The law set the standard of perfect righteousness, and all of humanity has failed to live up to that standard. The prophets testified to the spiritual failures of humans and longed for righteousness that seemed elusive and beyond their grasp.

When he came to earth and lived among humanity, Jesus Christ embodied God's righteousness, revealing what the law and the prophets had predicted. Although he is fully divine, he emptied himself of his lofty position, and came to earth in the form of a man. In becoming human but never sinning, Jesus addressed humanity's inability to measure up to the righteousness required to be in the presence of God's holiness. Since we could not go to where God is (heaven), God came to where we are.

God spanned the distance between humanity and himself through the work of Jesus Christ on earth, namely, his death and resurrection. His death abated the wrath of God toward our unrighteousness (the wrath described in the first two chapters of Romans), and the resurrection of Jesus demonstrated God's power over death. Since death is the ultimate consequence of sin, Jesus' resurrection showed God's power over the consequence of sin, as well as his power over sin itself. God solved the sin problem experienced by all humans (Jew and Gentile). Jesus died in our place as a sacrifice once and for all to satisfy the wrath of God on our behalf. Jesus is the revealed righteousness of God, but he then extends his righteousness to us.

A Righteousness from God is Received (3:22–23)

Romans 3:22 says that those who believe in Jesus are given the righteousness of Jesus. His righteousness cannot be earned; it is a gift. We receive his gift through faith. Faith is not some unknown mystical experience; it is trusting in God's provision for sin now, and future deliverance from sin in eternity. It is being certain of God's promises that cannot be quantified or seen with the human eye.

Faith is more than intellectual acceptance, although the intellect is involved in and affected by it. Faith is a living action, a personal conviction, and a trust and realized hope (Hebrews 11:1). Through faith, Jesus' righteousness is available to all people. In Romans 3:22–23, Paul used the word "all" to declare all people unrighteous (that is, they are sinners); he also declared that all people could be declared righteous apart from any work on their part. God's provision is universally available but not universally accepted.

Romans 3:23 is an often-quoted Bible verse, and it describes the definition of unrighteousness. Falling short of the glory of God describes humanity's inability to be declared innocent by verdict of the Eternal Judge, God. Although people may do right *sometimes,* no one can do right *all* the time; all people will eventually fall short of God's glory and standard. Falling short of God's righteousness leaves each person in need of a provision for God's wrath in response to that unrighteousness. Jesus offers us his righteousness to appease God's wrath, enabling us to experience peace with God.

A Righteousness from God is Restored (3:24–26)

These verses mention three terms that seem challenging to understand but contain rich theological meaning and significance: justification, redemption, and atonement.

All people need a restoration of our righteousness since we have all fallen short of God's glory. Because of his grace (giving us what we don't deserve), God offers a full restoration of our righteousness. The legal term that describes this process is *justification,* which simply means "the acquittal of unrighteousness." We have been *made right* in God's eyes even though we are not just or right. We are free from the penalty of sin and the guilt of sin. We did not earn this justification, but it was freely given to all who would believe. We are declared justified by grace, not by keeping the law (3:20).

Redemption is the legal transaction that results in our justification. It is the act of purchasing back something that once was owned, but that ownership was lost for a time. Leviticus 25 describes the redemption of a family member from slavery; it also describes the redemption of property. Christ's blood redeems us, or buys us back, from the power and penalty of sin.

When I was a child, my mother would get little green stamps with each purchase she made at the grocery store. When she collected enough stamps, she could redeem them for all sorts of items: cookware, small appliances, and even toys and gifts. That transaction was an exchange of one thing for another to receive an item of value. The price of the item had been pre-determined. Our redemption is similar. Our just and right nature is redeemed at a price—the very life of our

Savior. That's why Paul says we are bought with a price (1 Corinthians 6:20).

The price of our redemption is Jesus Christ himself. The legal term for that price is *atonement.* It comes from the Hebrew word *kaphar* meaning "to cover." It was an Old Testament term referring to the animal sacrifice at the altar that became the price of salvation for those who came to the temple. It is also the word used to describe the tar covering Noah's ark. The pitch sealed the survivors within the ark providing their physical salvation from the massive flood.

Even today, one person may say to another, "I've got you covered," while at a restaurant. This means that he or she will pay the bill for the other person. It means placing something over the other, covering any deficiencies the covered item might have. Jesus' perfect righteousness covers all of our spiritual deficiencies. Thus, he became our atonement, that is, the price that redeemed our righteousness and thereby justified us in the presence of God. When God looks at us, he no longer sees our sin but Christ's righteousness covering our sin.

Romans 3:26 points out that God demonstrated his own just and righteous nature in the face of our unrighteousness. We all deserve his wrath, but in his just yet loving nature, he extended his righteousness to us. By restoring our righteousness, God demonstrated that he is both just and the one who justifies.

A Righteousness from God is Realized (3:27–31)

Faith in Jesus is the sole means for receiving salvation, leaving no boasting in human accomplishment. God does the work of salvation in us. We cannot boast in anything we do. Our salvation and our righteousness are not based on the good we do—the observance of any moral code, our religious practice, or our religious heritage. Certainly morality, a godly heritage, and religious disciplines are good. Paul does not negate them or throw them away. However, they are the *product,* not the *basis* of the righteousness we obtain by faith in Jesus. How can we see ourselves any more privileged or better than anyone else?

Having this righteousness by grace through faith, we do not do away with the law; rather having this new righteousness, we start on our own journey of obedience and sanctification (becoming the holy people that God intends and empowers us to be). Having the righteousness of God revealed to us, then receiving it by faith and being restored, leads us to have a realized righteousness. In other words, the righteousness of God is not only a *legal status* gained from God, but also a *practical experience* we can have now. Jesus said so when he said that he came to give life and to give it abundantly (John 10:10).

Growing in Christlikeness by no means indicates that we can achieve perfection in this life (Paul detailed his own struggle with sin in Romans 7), but we can experience a freedom and joy in Christ because of the righteousness he has placed in our lives. This righteousness leads to a transformation of our minds (12:1–2) and to putting off the old, unrighteous self and putting on a new, righteous self (Ephesians 4:20–24). With this realized righteousness we can say with Paul, "Not that I have already obtained all this, or have already been made perfect, but I press on to take hold of that for which Christ Jesus took hold of me" (Philippians 3:12).

Implications and Actions

"The Roman Road" is a set of verses from the Book of Romans used to explain God's salvation in a simple manner. Although, there are variations, the following four verses can be used for sharing the good news of redemption with others:

1. Romans 3:23 declares that we are all sinners who have fallen short of the glory of God.

2. Romans 6:23 tells us that the wages of that sin is death.

3. Romans 5:8 affirms that while we were sinners, God loved us, and Christ died in our place.

4. Romans 10:9 offers the promise that if we confess the Lordship of Jesus in our lives and believe in our

hearts that God raised him from the grave, we will be saved.

Our unrighteousness separates us from God, but he revealed his righteousness to us through his word and ultimately through Jesus Christ. Jesus died as the atoning sacrifice to redeem us to God and to give us his righteousness by his grace. We can receive this as a gift through placing our faith in Christ. Have you accepted for yourself this free gift of grace? If you are not sure, or if you are certain you never have, would you receive God's gift of salvation today?

RIGHTEOUSNESS

Righteousness is a legal term in Greek (*dikaiosyne*), which means "a judicial verdict" or "approval." It is associated with justice, being found right, just, vindicated, or faultless in a matter. In divine terms, the word refers to the perfection and holiness of God, who is always just, right, and without fault. All people fall short of his perfection, unable to be righteous in every single action, thought, or word. Therefore, our "righteousness" is tarnished and incomplete.

Since we all continue to sin, we simply fall farther away from righteousness, never moving any closer to it. Some people believe that being right with God is a balancing act. They may say something like, "I think in the end when my good deeds are weighed against everything I did wrong, my good will outweigh my bad and that will be enough for God to let me into heaven." This is ill-informed theology. God's righteousness cannot tolerate our sinfulness. Each unjust act leads us farther from God, and no amount of moral living can bridge that gulf. Only God could remedy our lack of righteousness.

SIN

Romans 3:23 says that all have sinned. The Greek word for sin (*harmatia*) means "missing the mark." It is an archery term referring to missing the mark of a target. This understanding of sin is helpful in two ways. First, it reminds us that when we sin, we have missed the target of God's righteousness. Second, understanding sin as missing the mark keeps us from becoming proud. We may find another person who has missed the mark more, and we might feel we measure closer to God's righteousness until we realize that an archer can never be satisfied with a missed target, no matter how close he or she may come. In the best case scenario, a missed target (even by an inch) results in no points in an archery contest. It falls short of perfection. No matter what we do, we will fall short of God's righteousness.

QUESTIONS

1. Based on this lesson, define the following in your own words: righteousness, sin, justification, redemption, and atonement.

2. What is the difference between mercy and grace?

3. Describe the difference between earning God's righteousness and living in it by faith.

4. Explain how receiving salvation as a gift does not mean that we can continue to live an unrighteous lifestyle.

5. For further personal, in-depth study, research the term "imputed righteousness."

LESSON 5

A Faithful Example

MAIN IDEA

Abraham's life serves as an example of the necessity of faith.

QUESTION TO EXPLORE

How can we follow Abraham's example of faithful living?

STUDY AIM

To recognize that faith has always been the means of a right relationship with God and to choose to follow the example of Abraham

QUICK READ

Abraham was declared righteous by God before there was a law to obey and before the rite of circumcision was established. Therefore, God's promise of righteousness to Abraham and his offspring came by faith alone.

Introduction

We live in a *quid pro quo* (Latin for "something for something") world. I will give you something if you will give me something. I will scratch your back if you scratch mine. Very few things are given without getting something in return, whether it's recognition, affection, or honor. We grow up learning that we must earn our place in life. We must be good or talented or bright to earn any praise or reward.

This same *quid pro quo* attitude is the basis for legalistic religion. I do something good for God, and God does something good for me in return. I please God and God accepts me. I displease God and God rejects me. In today's focal passage, Paul used the faith of Abraham to illustrate how God's approval or acceptance of us is accomplished apart from works (our doing anything for him), and is imparted by faith alone (God doing everything for us).

ROMANS 4

¹ What then shall we say that Abraham, our forefather, discovered in this matter? ² If, in fact, Abraham was justified by works, he had something to boast about—but not before God. ³ What does the Scripture say? "Abraham believed God, and it was credited to him as righteousness."

⁴Now when a man works, his wages are not credited to him as a gift, but as an obligation. ⁵However, to the man who does not work but trusts God who justifies the wicked, his faith is credited as righteousness. ⁶David says the same thing when he speaks of the blessedness of the man to whom God credits righteousness apart from works:

⁷"Blessed are they

whose transgressions are forgiven,

whose sins are covered.

⁸ Blessed is the man

whose sin the Lord will never count against him."

⁹Is this blessedness only for the circumcised, or also for the uncircumcised? We have been saying that Abraham's faith was credited to him as righteousness. ¹⁰Under what circumstances was it credited? Was it after he was circumcised, or before? It was not after, but before! ¹¹And he received the sign of circumcision, a seal of the righteousness that he had by faith while he was still uncircumcised. So then, he is the father of all who believe but have not been circumcised, in order that righteousness might be credited to them. ¹²And he is also the father of the circumcised who not only are circumcised but who also walk in the footsteps of the faith that our father Abraham had before he was circumcised.

¹³It was not through law that Abraham and his offspring received the promise that he would be heir of the world, but through the righteousness that comes by faith. ¹⁴For

if those who live by law are heirs, faith has no value and the promise is worthless, [15] because law brings wrath. And where there is no law there is no transgression.

[16] Therefore, the promise comes by faith, so that it may be by grace and may be guaranteed to all Abraham's offspring—not only to those who are of the law but also to those who are of the faith of Abraham. He is the father of us all. [17] As it is written: "I have made you a father of many nations." He is our father in the sight of God, in whom he believed—the God who gives life to the dead and calls things that are not as though they were.

[18] Against all hope, Abraham in hope believed and so became the father of many nations, just as it had been said to him, "So shall your offspring be." [19] Without weakening in his faith, he faced the fact that his body was as good as dead—since he was about a hundred years old—and that Sarah's womb was also dead. [20] Yet he did not waver through unbelief regarding the promise of God, but was strengthened in his faith and gave glory to God, [21] being fully persuaded that God had power to do what he had promised. [22] This is why "it was credited to him as righteousness." [23] The words "it was credited to him" were written not for him alone, [24] but also for us, to whom God will credit righteousness—for us who believe in him who raised Jesus our Lord from the dead. [25] He was delivered over to death for our sins and was raised to life for our justification.

Works Won't Work (4:1–8)

In Romans 3:21–31, Paul laid out his argument for justification by faith and defended it against his critics. In Romans 4, Paul began by pointing out Old Testament (Jewish) Scriptures as precedent, using as examples the Jews' most prominent patriarch, Abraham, and the Jews' most prominent king, David.

The history of the Jews as God's chosen people did not begin with the giving of the law at Sinai; rather, it began with Abram (Abraham), with whom God entered into a covenant relationship that would affect the entire world (Genesis 12:3). Paul described Abraham as "our forefather according to the flesh," (Rom. 4:1, NASB) and one whose belief or faith was "credited to him as righteousness" (4:3). Thus, Abraham was not only a forefather of the Jews in an ethnic and familial sense, but also a forefather of all those who come to God in faith, both Jew and Gentile (Galatians 3:6–8).

The Jews considered Abraham the father of their race and the example of a faithful Jew. Paul used this argument to point out what made Abraham special before God. The question about what Abraham learned about righteousness apart from the law was asked in verse 1. Did Abraham discover that righteousness before God came through perfect obedience, such as the willingness to sacrifice his son Isaac (Genesis 22)? The Jewish people believed erroneously that Abraham achieved his standing before God because of his obedience to God on the mountain. Some religious people believe the same thing today: that only through obedience to God can a person be made righteous.

However, Abraham learned something quite different. He found out that the righteousness of God comes through faith and not works (Gen. 15:6). Some people today believe that in the Old Testament, people were saved by works, but in the New Testament and beyond, people were saved by faith. This misunderstanding leads some to believe that non-Jews are saved by faith in Jesus Christ, but Jews are saved by obedience to the Torah (the first five books of the Old Testament). All people come to Christ by faith through God's grace.

To help explain righteousness apart from works, Paul used the analogy of work and wages versus receiving a gift. When a person works, compensation is given in the form of wages, or what one earns. But if a person is rewarded without working, then compensation cannot be considered a wage; the wages are considered a gift. This gift or grace of God replaces the just punishment due to one who cannot live a perfect life. According to Paul in Romans 6:23, "For the wages of sin is death, but the gift of God is eternal life in Christ Jesus our Lord."

Paul reinforced this biblical understanding of righteousness apart from works by quoting David in Psalm 32. David had sinned against God by committing adultery with Bathsheba and by having her husband Uriah murdered (2 Samuel 11). David referred to his evil deeds as "transgressions" (*anomia,* which means "lawlessness"), and "sins" (*hamartia,* which can be translated as "failure"), because sin is both trespassing a boundary and falling short of a known standard. However, instead of holding our sins against us as a debt, God covers our sins and does not count them against us. This is righteousness apart from works.

Circumcision Not Enough (4:9–12)

The rite of circumcision is first recorded in Genesis 17:10–14. Circumcision was a sign of the covenant between God and Abraham, in which God promised to bless the world through Abraham (Gal. 3:8). Paul raised the question of whether the blessedness of God was intended only for the circumcised. Were the uncircumcised also included in God's promise? Paul raised this question because he has been arguing that righteousness came to Abraham apart from works, and that righteousness was credited to Abraham, not earned. Therefore, does God count circumcision as righteousness? And if so, is righteousness for the Jews alone? Or is it also for Gentiles?

Paul then led his readers through a timeline to demonstrate that Abraham was declared righteous *before* he was circumcised. God called Abraham in Genesis 12. God then declared Abraham righteous as recorded in Genesis

15. Fourteen years later, Abraham was circumcised as recorded in Genesis 17. Paul pointed out that circumcision was not the cause of Abraham being declared righteous before God, but was rather an outward expression of identification as God's chosen.

The apostles faced this controversy about circumcision in Jerusalem when some men came down from Judea to Antioch and taught that, "Unless you are circumcised, according to the custom taught by Moses, you cannot be saved" (Acts 15:1). Peter reminded the gathering that God chose him to proclaim the gospel to Gentiles so that they could be saved. He then declared, "God, who knows the heart, showed that he accepted them by giving the Holy Spirit to them, just as he did to us. He made no distinction between us and them, for he purified their hearts by faith" (Acts 15:8–9).

What did Paul mean when he said that Abraham received circumcision as a sign and seal of the righteousness that he had by faith? For Abraham, the sign of circumcision pointed to the existence of faith, and the seal of circumcision confirmed the genuineness of that faith. Abraham received the sign of circumcision, but that sign was a seal of the faith he had *before* he was circumcised. Because he had a righteousness by faith before circumcision, Abraham could be known as the father of all who believe but have not been circumcised.

Law Too Conditional (4:13–17)

If works don't work, and circumcision is not enough to produce righteousness, is obedience to the law sufficient? The promise of righteousness to Abraham came before the requirement of circumcision and hundreds of years before the giving of the Ten Commandments. Paul said that if those who depended on the law were heirs of righteousness, then faith meant nothing and God's promises to Abraham and his descendants were worthless. Paul explained that the law was never intended to bring righteousness, but only to reveal our sinfulness and our need of a Savior. Paul wrote in Galatians 2:21, "I do not set aside the grace of God, for if righteousness could be gained through the law, Christ died for nothing."

The word "promise" in Romans 4:16 refers to the covenant God made with Abraham in Genesis 17:2–4 and was fulfilled in Jesus. In Galatians 3:16, Paul wrote, "The promises were spoken to Abraham and to his seed. The Scripture does not say 'and to seeds,' meaning many people, but 'and to your seed,' meaning one person, who is Christ." Keeping the law is too conditional to bring righteousness. James wrote that if we break one of the commandments we have broken them all (James 2:10). Thus, righteousness must come outside of works or obedience.

Faith Just Right (4:18–25)

Some years ago, a Christian comedian envisioned what a baby shower invitation might look like for ninety-year-old Sarah. In one area are the gifts for the baby: pureed foods, a bib, gum ointment, and a walker. In another area were the gifts for the mother-to-be, Sarah: pureed foods, a bib, gum ointment, and a walker.

"Against all hope, Abraham in hope believed . . ." (4:18a). "Against hope" and "in hope" point in opposite directions. "Against hope" pointed to the impossibility of having a child at Sarah's age. In terms of natural human abilities, Abraham and Sarah could not pull off a birth. Abraham was without hope of having a child with Sarah.

"In hope," however, pointed to the possibilities of faith in God. This faith was not based on Abraham's external circumstances, but on the nature of God. Abraham believed in hope because God had promised offspring. Abraham attached his faith to the hope he had in God's promise, not in his or Sarah's abilities to procreate. He believed in God over believing in himself. He believed God could work the impossible. This belief of Abraham was "credited to him as righteousness" (4:22). Despite all his human flaws, Abraham was a man full of faith in God.

Paul connected Abraham's faith in God's promise of offspring with our faith in God who "raised Jesus our Lord from the dead" (4:24). This same Jesus was "delivered over to death for our sins and was raised to life for our justification" (4:25). The same God who promised and delivered offspring for Abraham, promised and delivered a Savior for all who would believe.

Abraham's example shows us that while works, circumcision, and the law could not bring righteousness, faith could provide the necessary right standing before God. "Consider Abraham: 'He believed God, and it was credited to him as righteousness.' Understand, then, that those who believe are children of Abraham" (Gal. 3:6–7).

Implications and Actions

What we learn from the life of Abraham (and to a lesser extent, David) is that God knows human perfection is not possible. God took two flawed men and used one to be the father of a great nation and of faith (Abraham); he used the other as an example of powerful and faithful leadership despite an inconsistent and sinful life (David). In using these two men, God demonstrated for us that his righteousness is a gift without strings attached. He made a covenant and promise with Abraham and completed it in the life, death, and resurrection of Jesus Christ. We receive the righteousness of God through faith in Jesus, apart from any good works.

This scriptural truth should free every believer from a sense of guilt and shame over sinful actions and the inability to live a life perfectly consistent with the law.

Our relationship with God through Jesus Christ does not depend on works, religious symbols, or religious behavior. It depends solely on God's promise of righteousness through faith in Jesus Christ.

CREDITED AS RIGHTEOUSNESS

One major difference between the Christian faith and other world religions is found in the word "credited" or "credits" in Romans 4:4–6. All other religions are based on works. Hindus affirm karma (deeds) and reincarnation. Jews depend on the law (works). Islam offers the five pillars (confession of faith, ritual prayer five times a day, giving a percentage of income, fasting, and pilgrimage). In contrast, Paul wrote, "faith is credited as righteousness" (4:5), and "God credits righteousness apart from works" (4:6). The word "credited" or "credits" comes from a Greek root word, *logizomai,* meaning, "to credit, to place to one's account, or to consider."

The basic idea of this word is that humans don't have enough good works in an account to please God and earn his love and forgiveness. Through the death of Jesus Christ for sin, God gives us forgiveness anyway. When a person quits working to please God for salvation, and instead places his trust in Jesus Christ for salvation, that trust or faith goes into one's personal account as a "credit" of righteousness.

APPLYING THIS LESSON TO LIFE

- Each day this week, look for examples of God's promises based in his grace and love, not good deeds.

- Put your hope in God for a hopeless situation in your life.

- Trust God to forgive a past sin that continues to make you feel guilty.

- Rest in God's promise of righteousness through faith alone. You can't earn God's love. He's already given it to you.

QUESTIONS

1. How can Christian disciplines (prayer, tithing, etc.) become a way of seeking to earn God's favor?

2. Why does keeping the law make us feel guilty?

3. Why is it hard for us to accept God's gift of righteousness unconditionally?

4. How can I apply hope against hope in my life?

5. In my daily life, do I trust in God's promises? Why or why not?

FOCAL TEXT

Romans 5:1–11

BACKGROUND

Romans 5:1–11

LESSON 6

Rejoice in Hope

MAIN IDEA

God's love, demonstrated in Christ's sacrifice, is the source of our hope.

QUESTION TO EXPLORE

Would you be willing to die for an enemy?

STUDY AIM

To grasp the depth of God's love and to experience the hope and joy he provides

QUICK READ

The love of God expressed in the sacrificial death of Jesus Christ for humanity's sin brings hope and joy. God transforms an enemy into a friend through this grace.

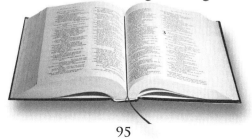

Introduction

Several years ago, I read a story about a young Army recruit at boot camp. His platoon had come in late after a long day of marching and hiking. Following dinner, they had turned in for the night. One young recruit was lying in his bed using a flashlight to illuminate his Bible as he read. His platoon leader took one of his muddy boots, threw it across the room, hitting the young recruit in the head while gruffly telling him to turn off the light and go to sleep.

The next morning the platoon leader rose early and saw something next to his bed that caused him to cry. Next to his bed were his boots, neatly cleaned and spit-shined. The platoon leader later shared this story and said, "What this young recruit did changed my heart."

In a much more grand and sacrificial manner, what God did for us through Jesus' death on the cross, even while we were his enemies, can change our hearts and fill us with joy and hope. That is the focus of this lesson.

ROMANS 5:1–11

[1] Therefore, since we have been justified through faith, we have peace with God through our Lord Jesus Christ, [2] through whom we have gained access by faith into this grace in which we now stand. And we rejoice in the hope

of the glory of God. ³Not only so, but we also rejoice in our sufferings, because we know that suffering produces perseverance; ⁴perseverance, character; and character, hope. ⁵And hope does not disappoint us, because God has poured out his love into our hearts by the Holy Spirit, whom he has given us.

⁶You see, at just the right time, when we were still powerless, Christ died for the ungodly. ⁷Very rarely will anyone die for a righteous man, though for a good man someone might possibly dare to die. ⁸But God demonstrates his own love for us in this: While we were still sinners, Christ died for us.

⁹Since we have now been justified by his blood, how much more shall we be saved from God's wrath through him! ¹⁰For if, when we were God's enemies, we were reconciled to him through the death of his Son, how much more, having been reconciled, shall we be saved through his life! ¹¹Not only is this so, but we also rejoice in God through our Lord Jesus Christ, through whom we have now received reconciliation.

The Witness of Grace (5:1–4)

Everything Paul wrote in the first four chapters of Romans paved the way for Romans 5. Paul used the word "therefore" in verse 1 to make a transition from his discussion in Romans 4. Because Abraham was not justified by works, circumcision, or the law, but by faith in the redemptive work of Christ, so everyone else is justified by faith alone as well.

The tense of the verb for justification (*dikaiothentes*) in this verse means that justification is an accomplished act, something that is finished rather than something that is pending or in progress. The problem of sin has been resolved in the death and resurrection of Jesus Christ. In Romans 5:2, justification provides "access" (*prosagoge*), meaning it brings us face-to-face with the grace of God in which a believer stands. The verbs "gained" and "stand" are in the perfect tense in the Greek, which means that their effect began in the past at the point of conversion, and the effect continues into the present (Ephesians 3:12). "Stand" carries the idea of something firm and lasting. To stand in grace means to possess a footing and anchor in God that can withstand all opposition to the life of faith. We have permanent access to God (Hebrews 4:16).

Peace, like justification, depends on God's action. Human beings cannot attain peace for themselves. The word "peace" (*eirene*) means to bind together that which has been separated. Peace is the result of being declared righteous, allowing us to stand face-to-face with God with no fear of his wrath or rejection. We are bound together with him again. God's wrath no longer threatens the believer. We are accepted in Christ. That brings peace.

The life of peace is not free from adversity; but adverse circumstances do not necessarily threaten the believer's peace with God. In verses 3–4, Paul spoke of struggle and suffering in the Christian life. The life of faith may result in adversity, but adversity is not necessarily a sign of divine judgment or abandonment. If justification produces release for the prisoner (and it does), peace is found in the life of freedom.

The Christian life is sometimes depicted in terms of triumph and success. However, Paul stated that the believer must learn to rejoice not only in the future hope of glory, but also in sufferings (5:3–4). He understood that present circumstances do not represent the final reality. This is a paradox because sufferings and afflictions appear to deliver us up to death, not to glory. But for Paul, faith enables sufferings and afflictions to display God's grace, not deny it.

Jesus suffered before he was exalted (Isaiah 52:13–53:12). The Apostle Paul's ministry led him to be persecuted and imprisoned often. In the early church, suffering was an essential part of the Christian's identification with the work of Jesus. Paul was not a proponent of the "health and wealth" gospel. He knew firsthand that the Christian life is one of "conflicts on the outside, fears within" (2 Corinthians 7:5, 11:32). He knew that suffering stripped away false securities and drove people to God for deliverance and hope.

The hope brought to each believer through the death of Jesus Christ inspires great confidence in God and his work in the believer's life. This hope or confidence in God should bubble over into joy in the believer's life. This hope can serve as an anchor for the believer, no matter the circumstances of life.

The Working of Love (5:5–8)

God has poured out his love into our hearts. The Greek word *ekchein* (poured out) suggests lavishness on God's part, like the occasional torrential rains that pour down in arid regions. One of the Holy Spirit's distinctive ministries is to pour out God's love on us. This overwhelming gift of God's love is the basis for our Christian hope. It was demonstrated most powerfully in Jesus' death on the cross. This love allows a believer to endure suffering.

What makes God's sacrificial love in Jesus Christ so amazing is its indiscriminate nature. Jesus died to save sinners. Jesus died for his enemies, not just his friends, as alluded to in John 15:13. This truth should cause believers to live humbly before others, whether they are Christians or not. We have no basis for being included as God's children other than God's love. Jesus showed God's attitude toward all of humanity.

Poor Richard's Almanac says, "God helps them that help themselves." This quote illustrates the erroneous idea that human beings must somehow contribute something in order to garner God's favor. However, Paul wrote that

God helps those who *cannot* help themselves. Jesus died for the powerless, ungodly sinners (5:8).

God demonstrated his love at "just the right time." Paul reiterated this truth in Galatians 4:4 when he wrote, ". . . when the time had fully come." This means the "appropriate time." In Romans 5:8, Paul used the Greek word *kairos* for the word "time" rather than the word *chronos. Kairos* denotes a favorable time or season, while *chronos* denotes chronological time, such as time on a clock or a twenty-four hour day. God operates on *kairos* time rather than *chronos* time. This is one of the reasons Jesus told his disciples in Acts 1:7, "It is not for you to know the times or the dates the Father has set by his own authority." *Kairos* time is God's time of opportunity.

The Welcome of God (5:9–11)

In verse 2, Paul wrote of the "hope of the glory of God." This is the hope of the believer's glorification at the end of life because of his sanctification through Jesus Christ. This hope is a promise of a glorious future made possible by the death of Jesus. This hope is not a wish (like hoping you win a new car), but rather a certainty based upon the fact that Jesus died for our sins. He changed us from the enemies of God to the friends of God, reconciling us with God.

Our justification by the blood of Jesus Christ means that we have been saved from God's wrath, saved through Jesus' life, and saved to rejoice in him. The assurance of salvation that the believer has in God through Jesus brings rejoicing (5:11).

Justification means being made right or being regarded as righteous in Jesus Christ. God grants justification as an objective state, not based on an inward feeling or attitude toward God. God's justification in Christ covers our past, our present, and our future. Justification is immediate, perfect, and permanent.

In reconciliation, God makes the sinner right with himself, which results in peace—peace of conscience, mind, and heart. In reconciliation, God did something for us and with us. The parable of the prodigal son (Luke 15:11–32) is a powerful illustration of reconciliation. Willfully defiant, the prodigal son left the father's house, made a mess of his life, and came home expecting humiliation and condemnation. Instead, the wayward son received what he did not deserve—shoes, a ring, a robe, a banquet, and most of all, his father's delight in receiving back the one who was lost but now was found.

Implications and Actions

When we consider the implications of God making us his friends through the death of Jesus Christ, we should be filled with hope and joy. At just the right time, the time when we needed God's acceptance, he sent Jesus to die for our sins. We did not establish this friendship and we will not be responsible for maintaining it. We trust the grace of God to maintain this friendship.

Because we are friends of God, we will never have to face his wrath. Jesus has faced God's wrath for us. Because we are his friends, we have hope even in the midst of suffering. We have hope and confidence that he is with us to help us persevere and build Christian character. His love is constantly lavished on us through his Holy Spirit. No matter who we are or where we are in life, God wants us to experience the peace and joy that results from his unrelenting love.

OUR INTERCESSOR

The word translated "access" in Romans 5:2, is the Greek word *prosagoge,* which means, "face-to-face." This verb occurs in only two other places in the New Testament, Ephesians 2:18 and 3:12. It could be translated as "introduction," which emphasizes that we are not fit to enter into God's presence. We need someone else to bring us in and introduce us. It was used to describe being granted an audience with a ruler or king.

In Hebrews 7:25, the writer explained that Jesus lives to make intercession for believers with God. The writer stated that this intercession or introduction can save us "completely." In Romans 8:34, Paul taught that condemnation no longer marks a believer's life because Jesus is at the right hand of God interceding for us. In addition, Romans 8:26–27 states that the Holy Spirit intercedes for us.

Through the grace of God, the believer is introduced as justified in a face-to-face meeting with God. The believer's justification is certified by Jesus and the Holy Spirit. Both members of the Godhead intercede continually for the believer.

CASE STUDY

Larry attended church with his family as a child living at home. He accepted Jesus Christ when he was ten-years-old and was baptized. When he went away to college, Larry gradually dropped out of church and hit the party circuit. He began to dabble in drugs, which led him further into an immoral lifestyle. He was eventually arrested and served several months in jail for possession of drugs. While he was in jail, a chaplain visited him. As he talked with the chaplain, Larry expressed doubts that he was still saved, that he was still God's friend. If you were the chaplain, what answer would you give Larry?

QUESTIONS

1. What causes me to doubt God's acceptance?

2. What is my greatest fear for the future?

3. How can I apply "standing in grace" to my daily life?

4. How does suffering cause me to question God's love?

5. What aspect of God's love brings me the most joy?

LESSON 7

Brought From Death to Life

MAIN IDEA

The gospel provides a path to life, not an excuse to sin.

QUESTION TO EXPLORE

Do we use the grace provided by the gospel as an excuse to sin?

STUDY AIM

To evaluate if I ever use the grace provided by the gospel as an excuse to sin

QUICK READ

The term "cheap grace" has been used to describe a believer who professes faith in Jesus Christ but does not live a life in obedience to the Scriptures.

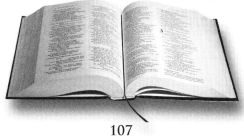

Introduction

A preacher once declared from the pulpit, "You can accept Jesus Christ, live like hell, and still end up in heaven." His point was that salvation depends on God's grace alone and not on human works. But is this what Paul meant when he wrote about salvation as a free gift of God?

Paul confronted the idea of cheap grace: I can be saved by a profession of faith in Jesus Christ, but my lifestyle doesn't have to change. He stated that believers in Jesus Christ should not offer themselves as active participants in the agenda of a sinful world. They instead should offer themselves as active supporters of God's agenda in God's world. This means continually surrendering themselves to God rather than pursuing a sinful lifestyle.

ROMANS 6

¹ What shall we say, then? Shall we go on sinning so that grace may increase? ² By no means! We died to sin; how can we live in it any longer? ³ Or don't you know that all of us who were baptized into Christ Jesus were baptized into his death? ⁴ We were therefore buried with him through baptism into death in order that, just as Christ was raised from the dead through the glory of the Father, we too may live a new life.

⁵ If we have been united with him like this in his death, we will certainly also be united with him in his resurrection. ⁶ For we know that our old self was crucified with him so that the body of sin might be done away with, that we should no longer be slaves to sin— ⁷ because anyone who has died has been freed from sin.

⁸ Now if we died with Christ, we believe that we will also live with him. ⁹ For we know that since Christ was raised from the dead, he cannot die again; death no longer has mastery over him. ¹⁰ The death he died, he died to sin once for all; but the life he lives, he lives to God.

¹¹ In the same way, count yourselves dead to sin but alive to God in Christ Jesus. ¹² Therefore do not let sin reign in your mortal body so that you obey its evil desires. ¹³ Do not offer the parts of your body to sin, as instruments of wickedness, but rather offer yourselves to God, as those who have been brought from death to life; and offer the parts of your body to him as instruments of righteousness. ¹⁴ For sin shall not be your master, because you are not under law, but under grace.

¹⁵ What then? Shall we sin because we are not under law but under grace? By no means! ¹⁶ Don't you know that when you offer yourselves to someone to obey him as slaves, you are slaves to the one whom you obey— whether you are slaves to sin, which leads to death, or to obedience, which leads to righteousness? ¹⁷ But thanks be to God that, though you used to be slaves to sin, you wholeheartedly obeyed the form of teaching to which you

were entrusted. [18] You have been set free from sin and have become slaves to righteousness.

[19] I put this in human terms because you are weak in your natural selves. Just as you used to offer the parts of your body in slavery to impurity and to ever-increasing wickedness, so now offer them in slavery to righteousness leading to holiness. [20] When you were slaves to sin, you were free from the control of righteousness. [21] What benefit did you reap at that time from the things you are now ashamed of? Those things result in death! [22] But now that you have been set free from sin and have become slaves to God, the benefit you reap leads to holiness, and the result is eternal life. [23] For the wages of sin is death, but the gift of God is eternal life in Christ Jesus our Lord.

Perish the Thought (6:1–5)

Romans 6 is divided up into two major sections. Verses 1–14 focus on freedom from sin, while verses 15–23 focus on freedom to obey God. Paul wanted to emphasize that grace does not equal the freedom to do anything because grace covers sin.

In verses 1–5, Paul argued against those who would teach that grace throws off all restraint from Christian discipline. Some people evidently saw grace as an opportunity to sin with impunity rather than seeing freedom from sin as the ability to live gratefully within the will of God.

The question Paul asked in verse 1, "Shall we go on sinning so that grace may increase?" evidently refers back to his assertion in Romans 5:20, "But where sin increased, grace increased all the more." The implication from his question is that a person is doing God a favor by sinning because he is giving God an opportunity to display more of his grace.

The phrase, "shall we go on sinning," comes from a Greek word *epimenomen*. The verb means, "to remain under." It is a present tense Greek verb that expresses continuing action. It carries the idea of remaining under sin habitually or continuing to sin. Paul answered his own question with the words in 6:2 when he said, "By no means!" In other words, "Perish the thought!" Paul did not want anyone to think that grace gives a person full license to sin. He explained that those who have believed in Jesus Christ have "died" to sin. A dead person cannot be tempted to sin; nor can he be ruled by a sinful nature. To die to sin means to die to the overpowering influence of a sinful lifestyle. A believer will still sin, but he or she will confess that sin and repent. John wrote in 1 John 1:9, "If we confess our sins, he is faithful and just and will forgive us our sins and purify us from all unrighteousness." This verse illustrates the repentant heart.

In Romans 6:3–4, Paul depicted baptism as a symbol of a dead person being buried in a grave and then being raised back to a new and different life. It is a symbol of the death, burial, and resurrection of Jesus. The Greek word for baptism in verse 3 is *ebaptisthemen*. It means literally, "to dip, immerse, or submerge." Baptists have traditionally followed the literal meaning of the word for baptism by immersing new converts, since it reflects more accurately a burial and resurrection. The New Testament believers trusted in Christ first and then were baptized as a symbol of the salvation process (Acts 2:41; 8:37; 9:18; 10:48).

Paul wrote in Romans 6:5 that the symbol of baptism, which shows that the believer has been united with Jesus in his death, also shows that the believer will be united with Jesus in his resurrection. This resurrection gives the believer the opportunity to live a new life.

Dying to Live (6:6–11)

Paul wrote in verse 6 that believers know from experience two things that non-believers do not know. First, our sin-bent old self was symbolically crucified and died when we repented and turned to Christ. Second, believers should no longer be slaves to sin. The "old self" refers to the believer before conversion. The Greek language uses two words for "old." *Archaios* refers to "old" in respect to time, and *palaios* means "old" with respect to use. Paul uses the word *palaios* in verse 6, indicating that the old self is worn out from sinful use and is to be discarded after conversion.

According to Paul, our old self was crucified with Jesus. Paul wrote of this again in Galatians 2:20, when he stated, "I have been crucified with Christ . . ." Paul saw himself as crucified on the cross with Jesus. For Paul, his body of sin, a body under the control of sin, died at conversion. In practical terms, it was made inoperative or inactive as a controlling influence. Conversion (turning to Christ) frees the believer from the control or domination of sin. The believer is no longer a slave to sin. One must die with Christ, or die to sin, in order to come alive to the life of righteousness. Paradoxically and symbolically, the believer dies in order to live.

In Colossians 2:13–14, Paul declared the sufficiency of Christ's death in defeating the power of sin, writing, "When you were dead in your sins and in the uncircumcision of your sinful nature, God made you alive with Christ. He forgave us all our sins, having canceled the written code, with its regulations, that was against us and that stood opposed to us; he took it away, nailing it to the cross." Paul called the death of Jesus a "sin offering" for sinful man (Rom. 8:3). Because of Jesus' sin offering and our conversion, we count ourselves dead to sin but alive to Christ.

Just Say No (6:12–14)

In verses 12–14, Paul wrote that believers needed to say "no" to the reign of sin in their physical body. They need to reject the use of their body for wicked activities and instead say "yes" to God and to offer their bodies as instruments of righteousness. The sinful nature will continue to try to usurp God's rule and authority through various temptations. To be tempted is not sin. Even Jesus was tempted (Hebrews 4:15). Giving in to temptation is sin.

We can remind ourselves that we are dead to sin and live in a redeemed state by saying "no" to the opportunities given to us to participate in a sinful lifestyle. Through a regular reading of the Scriptures and reliance on prayer and the Holy Spirit, believers remember and live in the new life found in Jesus Christ.

When Paul wrote, "do not let . . ." (6:12) and "do not offer" (6:13), he was acknowledging that the believer chooses whether or not to live the new or resurrected life. Believers must decide consciously to deny sin the opportunity to become a habit (to reign) or to become a lifestyle (offering the body over to wickedness).

Offering ourselves to God is an acknowledgment that God has delivered us from death to life. Living a Christian lifestyle by offering our bodies to perform righteous deeds is a sign of our gratitude to God for his gracious act of giving Jesus as a sacrifice for our sins. Paul wrote about this redeemed lifestyle in Ephesians 2:10, "For we are God's workmanship, created in Christ Jesus to do good works, which God prepared in advance for us to do." Identifying and using our spiritual gifts is one way of offering our bodies as instruments of righteousness. (See 1 Corinthians 12:1–11; Romans 12:6–8; Ephesians 4:11; and 1 Peter 4:10–11.)

Who is Lord? (6:15–23)

Paul closed this chapter with an appeal to believers to let loyalty to God rule in their lives, crowding out the lure of sin. A believer might be tempted to excuse sin, thinking that he is not under the law but under grace. Paul stated that the believer should never begin to think in this manner.

When a believer begins to rationalize that a little bit of sin is permissible, that thinking eventually leads a believer to becoming a slave to sin again. Paul pointed out that the believer has the choice to be a slave to sin which leads to death, or a slave to obedience (to God), which leads to righteousness or right living. What some have termed as "planned occasional sin" can lead to slavery to sin.

Historians tell us that during the medieval years, some leaders in the Catholic church wanted to raise money for the church. They taught that a person could purchase an indulgence, granting forgiveness for a sin in the past or in the future. In our day, people sometimes give large sums of money to the church in an attempt to pay for their future sinful behavior and appease feelings of guilt.

When Paul said that believers have been set free from sin and have become slaves of God, he was saying that believers have made Jesus the Lord of their lives. Jesus is now in charge of every day in every way. Making Jesus Lord leads to all the benefits of holiness (a life set apart to God).

Paul ended this section of Romans 6 with a comparison of the wages of sin and the gift of God. "Wages" referred to what someone earns for the work he performs. Giving self over as an instrument of wickedness for Satan's use results in the wages of death. However, when a person offers himself to God in faith to be made righteous, he receives a gift—eternal life in Christ Jesus.

Implications and Actions

Every person will serve someone or something. That service results in compensation. At some point in life, every person must decide whether they want to serve Christ or Satan. They determine to use their bodies for wickedness or righteousness. For the believer, that decision is influenced profoundly by their identification with the death and resurrection of Jesus Christ. The believer participates spiritually in the death and resurrection of Jesus Christ, and that identification with Christ gives him/her the power to live a new life in Christ. Rather than receiving the wages of death for being a slave to sin, the believer receives the gift of eternal life through Jesus Christ our Lord.

BAPTISM

The English word "baptism" comes from the Greek word *baptisma,* meaning "to dip, to immerse, or to submerge." It also means, "to identify with." When the Roman soldier was preparing to go to battle, he would dip his sword in blood identifying himself with the battle. When cloth was dyed, it was baptized (dipped and submerged) in a colorful liquid. When the cloth was brought up out of the dye, it had been identified with the color of the dye. Therefore, the physical act of baptism was a dipping, submerging, or immersion.

In the Bible, believers were baptized following conversion (Acts 2:41, 8:37, 9:18, 10:48). In Mark 1:9–10, the disciple wrote that John the Baptist baptized Jesus in the Jordan River, and that "Jesus was coming up out of the water," indicating that he was immersed in the river.

Paul wrote that the believer is identified with Christ's death, burial, and resurrection through baptism (Rom. 6:3–4).

CASE STUDY

A middle school student named Tommy was baptized by immersion in the local Baptist church. He couldn't wait until he got back to school to share this news with his classmates. One of his classmates named Richard told Tommy that he didn't remember when he was baptized because he was a baby when it happened. Tommy didn't understand how Richard could be baptized without making a decision to follow Christ. If you were Tommy's parent, how would you explain why Richard was baptized as a baby?

QUESTIONS

1. What occasional "planned sin" tempts you the most?

2. How is your life different since you became a follower of Jesus?

3. Where do you invest your life as an instrument of righteousness?

4. What influences you most to say no to sin?

5. What spiritual gift do you possess?

FOCAL TEXT

Romans 8:1–17

BACKGROUND

Romans 8:1–17

LESSON 8

A Spirit-Controlled Life

MAIN IDEA

Surrendering to the Holy Spirit provides life, peace, and affirmation of our adoption by God.

QUESTION TO EXPLORE

What are the characteristics and benefits of living a Spirit-controlled life?

STUDY AIM

To identify and embrace the characteristics and benefits of living a Spirit-controlled life

QUICK READ

Our sinful nature and the Holy Spirit vie for control of our lives. Surrendering to the Spirit produces life and freedom.

Introduction

It was my first summer missionary experience. The van from the mission center was only a few weeks old. Although I couldn't see the car behind me that had driven into the ditch to get around me, I discovered it was there as soon as the van's bumper collided with the car.

It wouldn't take too long to explain how the accident occurred, since it took place in front of the missionary who supervised me. And did I mention that a state trooper saw it all? The officer gave me a ticket, and perhaps fearing that I would flee instead of going to court, he confiscated my driver's license.

For weeks before my court appearance, I walked around bearing the guilt of my first fender-bender. Not just metaphorically mind you, since I no longer had my driver's license. I literally *walked* everywhere. I was not free to drive. Besides the guilt, I carried the burden of tarnishing my testimony as a summer missionary.

The only thing I remember from the court appearance was the judge returning my driver's license, scolding someone for taking it in the first place, and telling me that he would take the case under consideration. I never heard anything about the matter again. I never found out if the judge dismissed the ticket or if the missionary paid it. Whatever happened, I was not found guilty. I didn't have to pay the fine. The accident didn't follow me on my driving record. And I didn't have to pay for my newfound freedom. I look back on that summer with gratitude for the experience. It is also a reminder, on a very small scale, of the immeasurably great freedom we have been given in Christ.

ROMANS 8:1–17

[1] Therefore, there is now no condemnation for those who are in Christ Jesus, [2] because through Christ Jesus the law of the Spirit of life set me free from the law of sin and death. [3] For what the law was powerless to do in that it was weakened by the sinful nature, God did by sending his own Son in the likeness of sinful man to be a sin offering. And so he condemned sin in sinful man, [4] in order that the righteous requirements of the law might be fully met in us, who do not live according to the sinful nature but according to the Spirit.

[5] Those who live according to the sinful nature have their minds set on what that nature desires; but those who live in accordance with the Spirit have their minds set on what the Spirit desires. [6] The mind of sinful man is death, but the mind controlled by the Spirit is life and peace; [7] the sinful mind is hostile to God. It does not submit to God's law, nor can it do so. [8] Those controlled by the sinful nature cannot please God.

[9] You, however, are controlled not by the sinful nature but by the Spirit, if the Spirit of God lives in you. And if

anyone does not have the Spirit of Christ, he does not belong to Christ. ¹⁰ But if Christ is in you, your body is dead because of sin, yet your spirit is alive because of righteousness. ¹¹ And if the Spirit of him who raised Jesus from the dead is living in you, he who raised Christ from the dead will also give life to your mortal bodies through his Spirit, who lives in you.

¹² Therefore, brothers, we have an obligation—but it is not to the sinful nature, to live according to it. ¹³ For if you live according to the sinful nature, you will die; but if by the Spirit you put to death the misdeeds of the body, you will live,

¹⁴ because those who are led by the Spirit of God are sons of God. ¹⁵ For you did not receive a spirit that makes you a slave again to fear, but you received the Spirit of sonship. And by him we cry, ""Abba," Father." ¹⁶ The Spirit himself testifies with our spirit that we are God's children. ¹⁷ Now if we are children, then we are heirs—heirs of God and co-heirs with Christ, if indeed we share in his sufferings in order that we may also share in his glory.

Living Freely (8:1–4)

Our condemnation is a result of our sin and rebellion against a holy God. It is deserved. It is the result of a correct determination of our guilt. It is a just declaration.

However, the word carries a deeper meaning. More than mere guilt, "condemnation" includes both a guilty verdict and the subsequent punishment for that guilt. What a terrible combination for those who are bound up in sin: guilt, punishment, and condemnation.

Fortunately, not everyone experiences condemnation and punishment for sin. A divine adjudication has been made in God's spiritual courtroom. God, as the only rightful judge, has determined that instead of guilt, and in the place of punishment, there is now "no condemnation for those who are in Christ Jesus" (8:1).

Notice that the determination of "no condemnation" is not based on the sinner's actions. It's not that a person cleaned up his act so that judgment could be set aside. It's not that the sinner has made restitution or paid the debt that justice demanded. The declaration of acquittal has nothing to do with the sinner's action, but everything to do with the forgiven sinner's position in Christ.

Paul declared that those who turn to Jesus in faith are "in Christ Jesus." They are not "well-associated" with his followers or familiar with his history. They are not "in" a church building, a denomination, or a congregation, but *in Jesus.*

If you have ever jumped into the deep end of a pool, you know the sensation of being *in* the water. If you leap into the depths you become completely immersed in the water—there is water above you, below you, around you, and it may even be in you. (Close your mouth and wear earplugs!) When you are immersed in the water, it has consumed you. In much the same way, believers are immersed in Christ. Righteousness does not demand that we simply share Jesus' values. Holiness doesn't merely require moral improvements that inch us closer to Christ's example. We are immersed in Jesus to the point that we are consumed. "He must become greater; I must become less" (John 3:30).

The law was powerless to produce freedom and new life for humanity (Rom. 8:3). Righteousness required a sin offering, and God sent his Son to be that offering (8:3). Because the requirement of the law has been fully met in the person and work of Christ, there is now no condemnation for those who accept God's offering. All of the benefits of no longer being condemned are firmly grounded in Christ. We can be grateful for that. If my freedom is based on my ability to declare myself inno-cent, I will never experience freedom because the guilty cannot rightly declare themselves innocent. Rather, free-dom from condemnation rests on Christ's declaration, so we can be assured that he will not condemn us. Ever. His death in our place fulfilled the need for justice, so con-demnation and judgment are no longer necessary. Let the assurance of "no condemnation" empower you to live freely in Christ and for Christ.

If you are not living with this assurance, you can have it today. Jesus said, ""I tell you the truth, whoever hears my word and believes him who sent me has eternal life and will not be condemned; he has crossed over from death to life" (John 5:24). When you believe in Christ, you pass from death to life, from guilt to "no condemnation." You are no longer enslaved to sin; you are "set free from the law of sin and death" (Rom. 8:2).

The Spirit-Focused Life (Romans 8:5–10)

I enjoy thinking about some things more than others. I think about fishing much more often than I think about eating vegetables. Having my mind "set" on fishing might explain why I have several fishing rods and tackle boxes. It also explains why I don't own any gardening books or that amazing slicing, dicing tool promoted on late-night infomercials. Because my mind is not set on kale, I cannot distinguish it from collards. However, I can tell the difference between a red drum and a black drum when I reel it in.

Paul pointed out that those who live according to the flesh do not do so by accident. It is no coincidence that their lives are marked by, and driven by, sin. Living according to the flesh comes from having "their minds set on what that nature [the sinful flesh] desires" (8:5). When the mind is set on sexual satisfaction, life is lived in sexual depravity. Set the mind on selfishness, and greed will soon ooze out. Focus on the flesh and the mind will become governed by it.

The result of focusing on the flesh is death (8:6). A person focused on the flesh will become "hostile to God" (8:7). This hostility does not allow a person to submit to God. The fleshly mind neither wants to submit to God, "nor can it do so" (8:7). In this state, the flesh-focused mind "cannot please God" (8:8). This hostility and refusal to submit to God results in death.

However, the power of focus works both ways. Just like focusing on the flesh produces death, focusing on what the Spirit desires also produces fruit. "Life and peace" (8:6) mark the mind governed by the Spirit. The Spirit-focused life will be lived in sync with the Spirit (8:5) and will bring us life (8:10).

How can you have this Spirit-focused life? You must cross from the realm of the flesh into the realm of the Spirit. Without the Spirit, you do not belong to Christ and are still living in the flesh. You have crossed into the new realm "if the Spirit of God lives in you" (8:9). This can only take place when you turn from sin and turn toward Christ.

The Spirit-Empowered Life (Romans 8:11–14)

I heard the story of a man who owned a Volkswagen Beetle. He removed the engine in the little car and replaced it with a Porsche engine. You can imagine the looks he got as he passed others in a little, old car—not knowing that inside the car revved the power of a much greater racing machine.

Inside every Christian is power strong enough to raise the dead. Romans 8:11 describes who is living in every believer—the Holy Spirit. The Spirit raised Jesus from the dead. He (the Spirit) who gave life to Christ in the tomb "will also give life to your mortal bodies." This happens because of the Holy Spirit who lives in you.

When you own something powerful, you also own an obligation. If you own a power tool, you have an obligation to learn how to use it safely. If you own a rifle, the obligations are even greater. You must learn and practice safe storage, cleaning, and use. In a similar manner, the power you have received from the One who raised Jesus from the dead comes with a great obligation. What is this obligation? Paul made it clear that believers must turn away from the sinful nature and refuse to live according to it (8:12). Being obligated to the flesh would mean that we live according to the flesh. Living according to the flesh has a ruinous result—death (8:13). This would be in stark contrast to the Spirit's purpose of giving us life.

To the contrary, if believers live according to the Spirit, we "put to death the misdeeds of the body" (8:13). You will be a child of God (8:14) calling God "Abba, Father" (8:15). You and Christ are now co-heirs to the inheritance of God—an estate of sufferings and glory (8:17). If you can't believe your newfound status as God's beloved child, then believe the Spirit who "testifies with our spirit that we are God's children" (8:16).

Whether you live by the flesh or live by the Spirit, death will occur. Allow the misdeeds of the flesh to live on, and you will die spiritually. Alternatively, if you live by the Spirit, the misdeeds of the flesh will die, and you will live.

The choice is yours.

Implications and Actions

Trying to carry the burdens of sin and condemnation can be devastating. However, we can enjoy a permanent freedom from condemnation if we are in Christ Jesus. We cannot please him while we focus on the flesh. However, living by the Spirit produces life and peace that comes from the resurrection power of the Spirit in us. The Spirit in us brings about a spiritual adoption by which we become children of God with a divine inheritance. We must decide each day to be controlled by the Spirit and enjoy the fruit of a Spirit-controlled life.

No Condemnation

The word translated as "condemnation" in Romans 8:1 is *katakrima*. In short, it means punishment following condemnation. Outside of Scripture, it could mean punishment, damnation, or legal liability. *Katakrima* is found only three times in the Bible—in Romans 5:16, 5:18, and 8:1.

Paul placed a small, but powerful, word in front of *katakrima*. The word is *oudeis*, which means "not one." *Oudeis* categorically excludes whatever follows it. In this case, the modifier excludes condemnation. *Oudeis* is used to declare something as fact. The resulting reading of the phrase could be "not one condemnation in fact."

That the word *oudeis* comes at the beginning of Paul's sentence is important. New Testament writers placed words at the beginning as a way to bring particular emphasis to the word. Paul used all of the grammatical and literary tools at hand to make this declaration as forceful as possible. "No, as a matter of fact, there is now no condemnation— not one—for those who are in Christ Jesus!"

How would your life be different if you truly believed and acted on this verse?

CASE STUDY

Jim lived a life far from God. He readily admits that his mind was not set on God. He focused on drugs. As a consequence, Jim lost important things in his life, including his job, his family, his finances, his close friends, and his marriage.

Jim is now a Christian and strives to live a Spirit-controlled life. However, everywhere he looks, he sees the consequences of his past sin. He lives in a small apartment because he lost his job. He only sees his kids on the weekend. He cannot afford many "extras."

How could you help Jim understand his freedom from condemnation?

QUESTIONS

1. What are some things that "the flesh" desires?

2. What actions would you associate with a person living according to the flesh?

3. Have you seen how having the "mind set" on something changes a person?

4. Have you ever felt hostile to God? How was the hostility resolved?

5. How can we "put to death" the misdeeds of the body?

6. What does it mean to you to be able to call God "Father?"

LESSON 9

God Is For Us!

MAIN IDEA

God works for the good of
those who love him.

QUESTION TO EXPLORE

Do we really believe that God is for us?

STUDY AIM

To conclude that God is truly for me,
regardless of my circumstances

QUICK READ

From our present sufferings to
becoming more than conquerors, God
is at work for our good at all times.

Introduction

There's nothing like knowing that someone is on your side. Someone to console, encourage, defend, and take action on your behalf should the circumstances require it. You feel safer and more secure knowing somebody has your back. We are fortunate if we have a friend or two who embody such qualities.

How much more comforting it is to know that for those who have trusted Christ, the very God of the universe is on our side. Even when we can't see it or feel it, we can trust that God is always at work, orchestrating all things together for our good and his glory. He is for us!

ROMANS 8:18–39

18 I consider that our present sufferings are not worth comparing with the glory that will be revealed in us. 19 The creation waits in eager expectation for the sons of God to be revealed. 20 For the creation was subjected to frustration, not by its own choice, but by the will of the one who subjected it, in hope 21 that the creation itself will be liberated from its bondage to decay and brought into the glorious freedom of the children of God.

22 We know that the whole creation has been groaning as in the pains of childbirth right up to the present time. 23 Not only so, but we ourselves, who have the first fruits

of the Spirit, groan inwardly as we wait eagerly for our adoption as sons, the redemption of our bodies. 24 For in this hope we were saved. But hope that is seen is no hope at all. Who hopes for what he already has? 25 But if we hope for what we do not yet have, we wait for it patiently.

26 In the same way, the Spirit helps us in our weakness. We do not know what we ought to pray for, but the Spirit himself intercedes for us with groans that words cannot express. 27 And he who searches our hearts knows the mind of the Spirit, because the Spirit intercedes for the saints in accordance with God's will.

28 And we know that in all things God works for the good of those who love him, who have been called according to his purpose. 29 For those God foreknew he also predestined to be conformed to the likeness of his Son, that he might be the firstborn among many brothers. 30 And those he predestined, he also called; those he called, he also justified; those he justified, he also glorified.

31 What, then, shall we say in response to this? If God is for us, who can be against us? 32 He who did not spare his own Son, but gave him up for us all—how will he not also, along with him, graciously give us all things? 33 Who will bring any charge against those whom God has chosen? It is God who justifies. 34 Who is he that condemns? Christ Jesus, who died—more than that, who was raised to life—is at the right hand of God and is also interceding for us. 35 Who shall separate us from the love of Christ?

Shall trouble or hardship or persecution or famine or nakedness or danger or sword? [36] As it is written:

"For your sake we face death all day long;
we are considered as sheep to be slaughtered."

[37] No, in all these things we are more than conquerors through him who loved us. [38] For I am convinced that neither death nor life, neither angels nor demons, neither the present nor the future, nor any powers, [39] neither height nor depth, nor anything else in all creation, will be able to separate us from the love of God that is in Christ Jesus our Lord.

Glory: Nothing Compares (8:18–21)

Comparison is a part of life. As kids, we measured how tall we were compared to the other kids in our class. As students, we compared grades and clothes and then moved on to comparing cars, acne, and significant others. As adults, we compare opportunities, jobs, homes, waistlines, Christmas bonuses, and even our children's accomplishments (looked at Facebook lately?) Our compulsion to compare often produces negative results in our hearts and minds. When we compare and come out on top, we swell with pride. When we fall short, we struggle with anger, jealousy, insecurity, and greed.

The Apostle Paul talked about a different sort of comparison. He wrote, "our present sufferings are not worth

comparing with the glory that will be revealed in us"
(8:18). Our sufferings test us and seem to overwhelm
us. But Scripture explains the truth about our suffering,
including the importance of persevering under it. When
we focus on the glory that will be revealed in us, rather
than the immediate trials we are enduring, we are able to
look beyond the present to a time when suffering will be
nothing but a memory. After we have suffered—perhaps
a little, perhaps a lifetime—something extraordinary will
happen. God's glory will pierce through our suffering
and be revealed in us. Whatever we may be experiencing
in the present—brokenness, fear, shame, or pain—God's
glory will be revealed, and he will free us from these
difficulties.

God's glory will bring joy in the midst of suffering.
Peter challenged the early church to, ". . . rejoice that you
participate in the sufferings of Christ, so that you may be
overjoyed when his glory is revealed" (1 Peter 4:13). The
satisfaction and peace that come from understanding the
end result of our suffering can calm our current chaos.
The riches of Christ's grace will be sufficient. The depth
of his provision will meet each need.

You are not alone in waiting for this revelation of glory.
Creation joins you in expectation for the children of God
to be revealed (8:19). This same creation "was subjected
to frustration" (8:20). After Adam ate of the forbidden
fruit, God told him, "Cursed is the ground because of
you" (Genesis 3:17). At that moment, creation itself came

under the bondage and curse of sin. Yet, this frustrated but expectant creation is also hopeful that it "will be liberated from its bondage to decay" (8:21). Creation is looking forward to the future freedom when God's glory reigns (8:21b).

A Chorus of Groaning (8:22–25)

Creation responds to this frustration in much the same way that we do. It groans. Not the groan of having to sit through another boring meeting. Not the groan of facing a pile of work over the weekend. Not the groan of another bad play by your favorite football team. Creation groans "as in the pains of childbirth" (8:22). Creation itself, bearing the marks of sin, yearns and longs for a future time when it will again reflect the full glory of God.

Creation doesn't groan alone. Romans 8:23 declares that we have joined creation's groaning chorus as we ache inwardly for God's glory to be revealed. Do you remember times when you have been moved to groaning? A person beat you to the express checkout and doesn't notice or care about the "ten items or less" restriction. Groan. You pull up to the drive-through only to find eight other people with the same idea of a "quick" lunch. Groan. You tell the kids they can't open their presents until Christmas morning...big (seems like it will never end) groan.

These are insufficient examples to describe the angst that believers sense while waiting for Christ's return and his restoration of all things. If you have ever sat by the bedside of a loved one and watched cancer ravage his body, you have probably groaned inwardly with a deep desire for God's glory to become reality. If you have ever watched the news and listened to story after story of war, corruption, immorality run amuck, and blatant defiance of God, then you understand such groaning.

Our groaning and creation's groaning both express deep longing in the context of waiting. However, what believers wait for is different than what creation longs for. We "wait eagerly for our adoption" (8:23). That adoption is unique. Before the creation of the world, God chose us "to be adopted as his sons through Christ Jesus" (Ephesians 1:5). Those who receive him and believe in his name are called children of God (John 1:12). We have experienced God's grace and forgiveness, but we cannot enjoy fully all of the blessings that come from being called God's children until Christ's return. Some day, all those who have been called and justified will also be glorified (Rom. 8:30) and will experience the "redemption of our bodies" (8:23). We were adopted the moment we believed in Christ. We are in the process of being adopted. And yet we groan for the culminating glorification of our adoption. We hope for it and "we wait for it patiently" (8:25).

The Spirit's Wordless Prayers (8:26–30)

Creation groans. Believers groan. And the Holy Spirit groans. However, there is one clear distinction in relation to the Spirit's groaning. We groan because we wait, because we are expectant, and because we are hopeful. The Spirit groans not in anticipation, but in *intercession*. Paul wrote, "the Spirit himself intercedes for us with groans that words cannot express" (8:26). He intercedes for the purpose of aiding us in our weakness.

How is it possible that we are helped by an intercession we don't understand and can't even hear? Sometimes, prayerful communication comes very easily to us and our prayers seem to flow. Then we may face difficulties, times when we don't fully understand our circumstances, or comprehend the ramifications of our decisions. In those moments, when we can't understand what we're facing and we can't visualize our options, how can we know how to pray? Perhaps you have experienced a moment when you just couldn't verbalize everything you felt in your heart and thought in your mind. In those frustrating and agonizing moments, our weakness could be crippling, but it doesn't have to be. In our weakness, the Holy Spirit helps us. He intercedes for us by expressing those prayers that escape us—and he doesn't even need words.

Paul wrote, ". . . no one knows the thoughts of God except the Spirit of God" (1 Corinthians 2:11) and "he who searches our hearts knows the mind of the Spirit"

(Rom. 8:27). In a divinely unified way, the Spirit knows the thoughts of God and God knows the mind of the Spirit. Consequently, the Spirit need not even speak. Wordless groans can communicate to the heart of the Father what we need in our time of weakness.

The Spirit's prayers are not only wordless, but they are also perfectly synced. Because the "thoughts of God" and the "mind of the Spirit" are one in the same (because the Trinity is always in complete harmony), the Spirit's prayers for us are always "in accordance with God's will" (8:27). As the Spirit intercedes for us in keeping with God's good will, we can be confident that in every situation, God will work "for the good of those who love him" (8:28).

God Is For Us (8:31–39)

God is for Kimberly. God is for Ethan. God is for Jorge. Now add your name to that declaration: "God is for _____." Say it aloud. Does the statement sound unbelievable? Unreal? Implausible? Now imagine telling yourself and everyone else, "God is for me!" Would you feel embarrassed? Would you worry that others would say you are thinking too highly of yourself? God is for you. This may feel uncomfortable for you to say. It may be difficult to comprehend. But God has no problem with declaring it (8:31).

How can you know that God is for you? God has
shown his favor by what he has given to us. You may
be thinking about your life, your home, your career, a
prayer answered, or a loving spouse. Before he gave you
any visible, tangible gift, he gave you his only Son (8:32).
When the Father gave his utmost, he did so to assure us
that, along with his Son, he would "graciously give us all
things" (8:32). Because God has given you his best, you
can trust that he will give you the rest.

How else do you know that God is for you? Paul
declared that God called you (8:30) and justified you
(8:30, 33). Having justified you, who can condemn you?
The implied answer is emphatic: no one (8:34). Nothing
can condemn you. No person, no past sin, no judgmental
legalist, no well-meaning friend. God has justified you.
Declared you not guilty. Furthermore, the risen Christ is
now at the right hand of God and intercedes for you (8:34)
just as the Holy Spirit does.

Because God is for us, he has acted on our behalf. He's
given us his Son, justified us, and intercedes for us. All of
this gives us assurance in the face of hardship, persecution, famine, and sword. Nothing can separate us from
the love of Christ (8:35). In fact, God makes us more
than conquerors (8:37) and he makes the love of his son
Jesus to be inseparable from us (8:35, 39). God is for us,
which begs the question, "who can be against us?" (8:31).
Paul was convinced that nothing could separate God the
Father from his children— not death; not life; not angels

or demons; not powers; not anything else in all creation (8:38–39).

You can know that God is for you because he gave you his Son, chose you, justified you, set you free from condemnation, and now intercedes for you. He makes you more than a conqueror and permanently connects you with the love of Christ. There is plenty of evidence that God is for you. Do you believe it?

Implications and Actions

In making comparisons, it's important to compare "apples to apples" in order to get an accurate assessment of an item. However, in an "apples to oranges" comparison, Paul tells us that our present sufferings (apples) don't compare to the glory of God (oranges) yet to be revealed in us.

In confusing times of weakness, we can be encouraged that the Spirit of God intercedes for us. We can be confident that his prayers are in line with the will of God and will work for our good. As if we needed more assurance, God declares that he is for us. As a result, nothing can separate us from God's love, and this fact makes us more than conquerors.

God's glory will be revealed. The Spirit prays for you. Though all things are not good, all things will work out for your good and God's glory. God is for you. Christ's love is forever bound to you. Knowing all of these things, what do you need to do in response?

MISSIONARY SUFFERING & GLORY

In 1807, Adoniram Judson's career had an enviable beginning. He was the valedictorian of his class at Brown University. Within two years, he had made a profession of faith and soon became interested in missionary efforts.

Adoniram arrived in India in 1812 and was baptized at the Baptist Church of Calcutta. Unfortunately, he was forbidden from doing any missionary work there. A year later, he landed in Burma and began his missionary work. Adoniram worked for six years before he saw the first convert under his ministry.

These roadblocks were only the beginning of a tumultuous life. He spent seventeen months in prison. For nine of those months, Adoniram was bound with three pairs of fetters (heavy chains binding the feet). He suffered hunger, heat, and illness under cruel captors. Adoniram's wife Ann died during this time. His second wife died on his visit home after thirty years of service.

Before he died at sea, Adoniram was asked how bright the prospects were for the conversion of the world. Believing God's glory to be revealed, he said "As bright, sir, as the promises of God."[1]

CASE STUDY

Olivia feels like everything and everyone is against her. At home, her mom takes her sister's side all the time. Her dad is always on her case about homework, her cell phone, or doing chores. Olivia sits alone during lunch and believes no one wants to be her friend. Even at church, she doesn't feel as connected or accepted as the other students in her group. How could you help Olivia understand that God is for her, even though it seems as if everyone and everything is against her?

QUESTIONS

1. How do you feel your sufferings compare with the sufferings of others?

2. How have you seen the glory of God revealed in your life?

3. What do you think it means to "groan inwardly?"

4. Have you ever been at a loss for words in your prayers? Explain.

5. What helps you to pray "in accordance with the will of God?"

6. What can you point to that shows that God is for you?

NOTES ———————————————————————

1. http://www.mocavo.com/The-New-Schaff-Herzog-Encyclopedia-of-Religious-Knowledge-Volume–6/365646/281. Accessed 12/19/2014.

FOCAL TEXT
Romans 9:1–8; 10:1–21

BACKGROUND
Romans 9—11

LESSON 10

God's Choice and Our Responsibility

MAIN IDEA

God chose to reveal himself through Israel, and everyone who chooses him will be saved.

QUESTION TO EXPLORE

What is the difference between hearing the gospel and responding to it?

STUDY AIM

To understand that the proper response to the gospel is individual trust and confession, not a reliance on religious heritage.

QUICK READ

In the past (like today), a perfect God revealed himself to and through an imperfect people. Some of the Israelites believed while others did not. We, too, must choose whether or not to follow him.

Introduction

When I heard the sirens go off, I felt like I needed to run. But I didn't know where to run. I didn't even know why I would be running. I was confused. I was nervous. I'll admit it, I was afraid. At the time, I was making one of many presentations on the subject of company retirement plans. The presentations were not for just any employees; these were federal contractors who worked in a plant where munitions were disassembled. Translation: *they were taking bombs apart.* And an alarm had just gone off while I was on-site.

I looked down at the security tag I had been given when I arrived. It listed information about what to do in case of an alarm. If the alarm sound was a warble, it meant one danger. If it was continuous, it represented a different issue. The missing piece of information? What to do in case the alarms blared. I had information. What I needed were instructions!

The alarm wasn't tripped by uranium leakage or unstable explosives, I later learned. Rather, the sensors in the facility were so sensitive that too much perfume or cologne could set off alarms. A few particulates of perfume had made their presence known to the entire fortified facility. I could not see the perfume drops, but their presence was ear-shatteringly obvious. In much the same way, you and I may not see God like we see a building or another human being, but he has made his presence known throughout history. Our challenge is to make the proper response to God's revelation.

ROMANS 9:1–8

[1] I speak the truth in Christ—I am not lying, my conscience confirms it in the Holy Spirit— [2] I have great sorrow and unceasing anguish in my heart. [3] For I could wish that I myself were cursed and cut off from Christ for the sake of my brothers, those of my own race, [4] the people of Israel. Theirs is the adoption as sons; theirs the divine glory, the covenants, the receiving of the law, the temple worship and the promises. [5] Theirs are the patriarchs, and from them is traced the human ancestry of Christ, who is God over all, forever praised! Amen.

[6] It is not as though God's word had failed. For not all who are descended from Israel are Israel. [7] Nor because they are his descendants are they all Abraham's children. On the contrary, "It is through Isaac that your offspring will be reckoned." [8] In other words, it is not the natural children who are God's children, but it is the children of the promise who are regarded as Abraham's offspring.

ROMANS 10:1–21

[1] Brothers, my heart's desire and prayer to God for the Israelites is that they may be saved. [2] For I can testify about them that they are zealous for God, but their zeal is not based on knowledge. [3] Since they did not know the righteousness that comes from God and sought

to establish their own, they did not submit to God's righteousness. ⁴Christ is the end of the law so that there may be righteousness for everyone who believes.

⁵Moses describes in this way the righteousness that is by the law: "The man who does these things will live by them." ⁶But the righteousness that is by faith says: "Do not say in your heart, 'Who will ascend into heaven?' " (that is, to bring Christ down) ⁷"or 'Who will descend into the deep?' " (that is, to bring Christ up from the dead). ⁸But what does it say? "The word is near you; it is in your mouth and in your heart," that is, the word of faith we are proclaiming: ⁹That if you confess with your mouth, "Jesus is Lord," and believe in your heart that God raised him from the dead, you will be saved. ¹⁰For it is with your heart that you believe and are justified, and it is with your mouth that you confess and are saved. ¹¹As the Scripture says, "Anyone who trusts in him will never be put to shame." ¹²For there is no difference between Jew and Gentile—the same Lord is Lord of all and richly blesses all who call on him, ¹³for, "Everyone who calls on the name of the Lord will be saved."

¹⁴How, then, can they call on the one they have not believed in? And how can they believe in the one of whom they have not heard? And how can they hear without someone preaching to them? ¹⁵And how can they preach unless they are sent? As it is written, "How beautiful are the feet of those who bring good news!"

¹⁶ But not all the Israelites accepted the good news. For Isaiah says, "Lord, who has believed our message?" ¹⁷ Consequently, faith comes from hearing the message, and the message is heard through the word of Christ. ¹⁸ But I ask: Did they not hear? Of course they did:

> "Their voice has gone out into all the earth,
>   their words to the ends of the world."

¹⁹ Again I ask: Did Israel not understand? First, Moses says,

> "I will make you envious by those who are not a
>   nation;
> I will make you angry by a nation that has no
>   understanding."

²⁰ And Isaiah boldly says,

> "I was found by those who did not seek me;
> I revealed myself to those who did not ask for
>   me."

²¹ But concerning Israel he says,

> "All day long I have held out my hands
> to a disobedient and obstinate people."

God Revealed (9:1–9)

In chapters 1—8 of Romans, Paul addressed great truths about the interaction between God and humanity. He spoke about the pervasive nature of sin, declaring that every person has sinned and fallen short of God's glory.

Paul spoke about the extent of God's love for us demonstrated when Christ died for us while we were still sinners and enemies of God (5:8). He described the universality of sin (3:10) and universality of the gospel, available to every person despite heritage, race, or birthright (1:16). In Romans 12—15, the Apostle Paul instructed the church on how to interact with God (12:1); each other (12:5, 9); the governing authorities (13:1); creditors (13:7); and people with different beliefs and practices (14; 15:1-13).

Sandwiched in between these bookends fall chapters 9—11, in which Paul described how God interacted with the Jewish people throughout history. God showed the people of Israel sonship, divine glory, covenants, and temple worship (9:4). God also gave them the law and his promises. Not only did the patriarchs of the Jewish faith come from the Israelites, but they could also make a unique claim: "from them is traced the human ancestry of Christ, who is God over all" (9:5). No other race could trace its roots to the Messiah, the hope of Israel.

What is the unifying premise for this entire section? The premise that God's invisible qualities—including his power and divinity—have been clearly visible in creation. People can look at a sunset and deduce that divinity was behind the masterpiece. Because God has made himself known throughout history, no one can make an excuse for not believing in him (1:20). Rather than remaining distant from his creation, God chose to reveal himself through the law and the prophets, proclaiming a trove of concepts with divine consequence, including sin, condemnation, salvation, love, mercy, and sanctification.

Imperfect Vessels (10:1–13)

How could God make divine principles palpable to people? How could God explain principles like justice, love, mercy, holiness, and salvation? In the Old Testament, he used the Jewish people—the Israelites. He demonstrated favor, love, mercy, and other concepts to the Jewish people, and God expected those people to live differently than others on the planet who did not experience this divine love. People from other nations came into contact with God's chosen people. God wanted these foreign nations to know immediately that his people had something they did not—the presence of God himself.

One limitation in this divine revelation, however, is that a perfect God chose to work with broken vessels. Whether God chose the Jews, the Canaanites, the Egyptians, or even you and me, the whole of humanity are broken vessels. In writing to the Roman people, Paul noted the deficiencies in the Jewish people. Their zeal was misdirected (10:2). Not all of them accepted the good news (10:16). Some failed to understand (10:19). Many were "disobedient and obstinate" (10:21). The Israelites' varied response to God's love illustrates how each person can choose whether or not to accept and respond positively to his overtures of grace.

"All have sinned" (3:23) and among us there is not even one who is righteous (3:10). We have followed in Israel's rebellious footsteps. We share in the same condemnation—death (6:23). However, just as the Jews could have claimed, we claim God's righteousness for our own. Paul said that righteousness is "possible for everyone who believes in the Messiah" (10:4). For Jews and Gentiles alike, and for you and for me, the promise is the same. If we confess Christ as Lord and trust in his death and resurrection as our redemption price, we will be saved (10:9).

Your ancestors probably don't trace their lineage to the line of David or to those who saw miracles in the desert. You may not be able to trace your family heritage back to Abraham, Isaac, or Jacob. A religious pedigree is not required of those who desire a right relationship with God through Jesus Christ. Paul could not be more clear or emphatic. "For there is no difference between Jew and Gentile—the same Lord is Lord of all and richly blesses all who call on him" (10:12). Have you been richly blessed by God because you asked him for mercy and forgiveness? Call on him today and receive the richest blessing of all—to be saved from the just punishment for your sin.

An Imperfect Analogy (10:14–21)

Calling on the name of the Lord for salvation requires belief, hearing, preaching, and a proclaimer (10:14–15). Those whom God sent with "beautiful feet" to "bring good news" included prophets, priests, and kings throughout Israelite history. However, the ultimate bearer of good news was his Son, Jesus. Unfortunately, not all Israelites accepted the good news (10:16).

Imagine a small bottle of perfume. What would happen if the contents were dispersed throughout an entire football stadium? Such a volume of air would lessen the impact of the perfume. Add to that the smells of hot dogs, popcorn, a field full of sweaty football players and an entire stadium full of people. Those elements would make the perfume's scent almost imperceptible. Someone smelling the scent might only get a faint representation of the concentrated perfume. The aroma is stronger and more distinct when the droplets are held together.

In much the same way, God chose to reveal himself, to pour himself out (like a perfume) on all creation. God created every person uniquely to show part of the *imago dei*—the image of God. Each person reflects merely a hint of him. Like those perfume droplets dispersed throughout the football stadium, the image of God is dispersed throughout all of humanity. Our sinfulness is to God's revelation as the stinky stadium is to the perfume. The pervasive sinfulness of each individual makes it difficult to see the image of God in human beings. Like the perfume, the aroma is more perceptible when it is concentrated. God selected the Jewish people to be the perfume bottle that would hold a concentration of his revelation. In the personal lives of the people and the collective life of the nation, God would focus his work, his declarations, his manifestations, and his expectations. Like all other people, the nation of Israel was not a perfect vessel, yet God chose to reveal himself through them.

The perfume and bottle analogy falls short in many respects. We cannot grasp what God does, how he does it, and why he chooses to act. We may find "unsearchable his judgments, and his paths beyond tracing out!" (11:33). However, we can grasp enough of him to respond to him. We have seen God revealed initially through his creation and his chosen people, Israel. We see God revealed perfectly through his Son. We pray for others to see God revealed in us through his Spirit. While we wait for the time when we will see him completely and gloriously, may our mouths and lives declare God's glory (11:36) and not our own.

Implications and Actions

God is beyond understanding, yet he chose to reveal himself to humanity. He chose the nation of Israel to be the initial conduit of that revelation. Although imperfect,

Israel was uniquely utilized to reveal great truths, prophesies, and promises. God's revelation had begun, but it was limited by the disobedience of human beings. Later, God revealed himself wholly and perfectly through Christ. In him, both Jews and Gentiles can call on the same Lord and be saved. Like Israel, we must choose to believe and to obey. We must choose to allow God to use our lives to reveal himself to others around us.

MISDIRECTED ZEAL

In Romans 10:2, Paul offered himself as a personal witness of the Israelites' "zeal for God." Paul used the word *zelos* when referring to the attitude of those he prayed would be saved. *Zelos* could refer to ardor, zeal, or jealousy. Its root word, *zeo*, means "to be hot, to boil."

These definitions are evident in Jesus' description and warning of the teachers of the law and the Pharisees in Matthew 23. These men were so zealous they would "travel over land and sea to win a single convert" (Matt. 23:15), tithe their spices (23:23), and carefully followed cleanliness with their dishware (23:25). They were jealous of their social status (23:6) and titles (23:7).

Despite their religious show, Jesus had harsh words for them. He called them hypocrites (Matt. 23:13–37), snakes, a brood of vipers (23:33), and blind guides (23:16). Their zeal was wrapped up in their human religious rules rather than loving God wholeheartedly. No wonder Paul described the Jews' *zelos* as being mistaken (Rom. 10:3). Zeal is good as long as it is based on knowing Christ and understanding how his sacrifice makes our righteousness possible.

Case Study

Mercy takes special pride in the church building. She volunteers weekly to clean it; she heads up the decoration committee; she always wants "her Father's house" to look its best. Vacation Bible School started this week. The church bus is bringing unchurched kids to participate. Mercy is glad they hear the gospel, but she does not like how they track in mud on the new carpet, spill their refreshments, color on the tables, and make a mess in general. She finds their language and their manner of dress disrespectful. Their behavior makes her mad, and it shows in her attitude and interactions with the children. How can you help Mercy temper her zeal for the church with a greater zeal for the gospel?

QUESTIONS

1. Why do you think God chose to reveal himself *to* people *through* people?

2. What did God reveal through Israel that is applicable to us today?

3. Which of Israel's shortcomings and acts of disobedience (mentioned by Paul) have you and I also committed?

4. According to Romans 10:9–13, what things do Jews and Gentiles have in common?

5. What happened the first time someone told you the "good news" of Jesus Christ?

LESSON 11
A Lifestyle of Worship

MAIN IDEA

Our response to the gospel should result in a lifestyle of worship.

QUESTION TO EXPLORE

How can I pursue a lifestyle of worship?

STUDY AIM

To offer myself to God as a living sacrifice, exercising my spiritual gifts in love.

QUICK READ

We live a life of worship by renewing our minds, using our spiritual gifts, and sincerely loving one another.

Introduction

One of the greatest sinners wrote one of the greatest hymns. John Newton, the author of "Amazing Grace," was only eleven-years-old when he was drafted into the British Navy. After being dismissed for insubordination, Newton became the captain of a slave ship. He left the slave trade after his dramatic conversion at sea and became an ardent advocate for the abolition of slavery. God's mercy and grace transformed Newton's life.

John Newton never forgot the power of God's transforming grace. He became a well-known evangelical preacher, but his influence extended far beyond the pulpit. Newton encouraged William Wilberforce in William's forty-year fight against slavery, and Newton himself testified in Parliament about the horrors of the slave trade. John Newton didn't just write songs about worship. He lived worship.

Experiencing God's amazing grace should prompt our sincere worship, but worship is not just singing songs and listening to God's word on Sunday mornings. Worship is a pattern and a lifestyle. Like Newton, we are called to do more than sing songs of worship. We are called to live a life of worship.

ROMANS 12

1 Therefore, I urge you, brothers, in view of God's mercy, to offer your bodies as living sacrifices, holy and pleasing to God—this is your spiritual act of worship. 2 Do not conform any longer to the pattern of this world, but be transformed by the renewing of your mind. Then you will be able to test and approve what God's will is—his good, pleasing and perfect will.

3 For by the grace given me I say to every one of you: Do not think of yourself more highly than you ought, but rather think of yourself with sober judgment, in accordance with the measure of faith God has given you. 4 Just as each of us has one body with many members, and these members do not all have the same function, 5 so in Christ we who are many form one body, and each member belongs to all the others. 6 We have different gifts, according to the grace given us. If a man's gift is prophesying, let him use it in proportion to his faith. 7 If it is serving, let him serve; if it is teaching, let him teach; 8 if it is encouraging, let him encourage; if it is contributing to the needs of others, let him give generously; if it is leadership, let him govern diligently; if it is showing mercy, let him do it cheerfully.

9 Love must be sincere. Hate what is evil; cling to what is good. 10 Be devoted to one another in brotherly love. Honor one another above yourselves. 11 Never be lacking in zeal, but keep your spiritual fervor, serving the Lord.

12 Be joyful in hope, patient in affliction, faithful in prayer.
13 Share with God's people who are in need. Practice hospitality.

14 Bless those who persecute you; bless and do not curse. 15 Rejoice with those who rejoice; mourn with those who mourn. 16 Live in harmony with one another. Do not be proud, but be willing to associate with people of low position. Do not be conceited.

17 Do not repay anyone evil for evil. Be careful to do what is right in the eyes of everybody. 18 If it is possible, as far as it depends on you, live at peace with everyone. 19 Do not take revenge, my friends, but leave room for God's wrath, for it is written: "It is mine to avenge; I will repay," says the Lord. 20 On the contrary:

"If your enemy is hungry, feed him;
      if he is thirsty, give him something to drink.
      In doing this, you will heap burning coals on his
         head."

21 Do not be overcome by evil, but overcome evil with
      good.

Worship Through the Renewing of Our Minds (12:1–2)

The first eleven chapters of Romans are deeply theological, wrestling with the truth and implications of the gospel. In Romans 12, Paul turned the conversation to a more practical tone, first writing about living out the gospel. Worship is the appropriate response to God's deep and rich mercy.

Paul told the Roman believers who had experienced God's mercy to offer their bodies as "living sacrifices" (12:1). Both Gentile and Jewish believers in Paul's day would have understood the reference to sacrifice. Animal sacrifice was an integral part of both pagan rites and the Jewish faith. To offer one's self as a sacrifice was Paul's way of telling his readers to give every part of themselves to the Lord. You can't just sacrifice part of a sheep; sacrifice requires an "all-or-nothing" commitment. Similarly, believers are called to give their whole selves—physical, emotional, mental, and spiritual—to the Lord. God doesn't just want our tithes or our Sunday morning attention. God wants all of us, and he deserves nothing less.

As we commit ourselves to the Lord, he transforms us to become more like Christ. This change must begin with our minds because how we think shapes what we do. The world has its own pattern of thinking, promoting every evil idea and selfish approach to life. The world teaches that you can do whatever you want as long as nobody gets hurt. Unfortunately, the world doesn't understand that sin always results in pain.

A renewed mind thinks new thoughts that are based on the truth found in the Bible, not the world's system of belief. We begin to see the world the way God does and think as he does (Isaiah 55:8–9; 1 Corinthians 2:16).

We admit our sin instead of making excuses for it. We strive for holiness instead of compromising. We love our enemies instead of hating them, and we seek justice and mercy instead of revenge. As we think differently, we will live differently, and we will start to reflect the character of Jesus.

We renew our minds by encountering God in Scripture. Some believers try to make the Bible conform to their ideas and beliefs. They ignore verses or rationalize away passages they don't like or ones that would cause them to make radical changes in their lives. Such arrogance denies the authority of Scripture and puts human ideas above God-given truth. At times, we as believers may have to grapple with Scripture and wrestle with how to apply its truths to our lives, but we don't get to dismiss or rewrite the parts that challenge us or call us to repentance. The Bible is not meant to conform to our beliefs. We are meant to conform ourselves to it.

As we renew our minds and learn to think how God thinks, we become better able to discern the will of God. As we learn to think the way God does about our neighbors, our world, and ourselves, we know what pleases him. The transformation of our minds allows us to both identify and live out God's will in our lives. This continual renewal allows us to live a life of worship.

Worship by Exercising My Spiritual Gifts (12:3–8)

The transformation of our minds produces worship, and we live out that worship in the context of the community of faith. In verse 3, Paul warned believers against thinking too highly of themselves, and he challenged them to see themselves with "sober judgment," that is, to see themselves in proper perspective to God. Our goal as living sacrifices is to make much of Jesus, not to draw attention to ourselves.

True worship begins when Jesus is the focus of our lives—not our pride, desires, or reputation. Romans 6:3 warns believers against measuring themselves against others in order to determine their worth. We all stand on level ground at the foot of the cross, equally needing God's mercy and grace. As fellow recipients of God's love, we all work together for *his* glory in a spirit of cooperation, not competition.

In these verses, Paul compared the church to the physical body. Just as a physical body needs every part working properly for it to function well, the church needs each person to use his or her spiritual gifts for the church to function as God intended. The word Paul used for "gifts" is *charismata,* which comes from the Greek word for "grace," or *charis.* Our spiritual gifts are gifts of God's grace. We should not be proud about the gifts granted to us. Nor should we use our gifts to elevate ourselves, just as the liver should not consider itself more essential than the kidneys. Every spiritual gift—and every person in the body of faith—is essential and vital.

We worship God by serving him, using our gifts in service to his church. The pastor and the praise team are not the only worshippers on Sunday morning. Whether we serve in the nursery, greet people in the parking lot, teach a Sunday school class, or vacuum the carpet after everyone has gone home, we are actively worshipping God. Our worship also extends into the community. When we write an encouraging note to a police officer, deliver a meal to the sick friend, volunteer at the literacy center, or give a person a second chance, we are worshipping. The Spirit of God works through us as we use the grace-gifts God has given us, and we live a life of worship.

Worship by Loving Others Sincerely (12:9–21)

A life of worship is also reflected in our relationships with others. In verse 9, Paul told believers to love each other sincerely. The word translated as "love" is *agape,* the Greek word used to describe God's unconditional love. It is love expressed in action. Sincere love both hates evil and clings to what is good (12:9). Real love does not tolerate evil; it despises sin because it destroys lives. The love underlying all biblical ethics is not a wishy-washy, passive, compliant emotional soup. Love is active. It fights evil and it clings to what is good, because love always seeks the best for each person.

Paul also told the Roman church "to be devoted to one another in brotherly love" (12:10). In verse 10, Paul used the Greek word *phileo,* which is translated as "brotherly love." In doing so, Paul inferred that the church is like a family; believers are called to show sincere concern and affection for each other. We must fight against apathy, encouraging one another to not grow weary in doing good. We remind one another that because Jesus gave us fullness of joy, we can be joyful even when life gets hard (John 15:11). Because God has been generous to us, we can demonstrate generosity toward others. We don't let messy rooms and dirty dishes keep us from throwing open the front door and welcoming others into our homes and our lives. Our actions show our love for one another, and together we live a life of worship.

Our love is not limited to our friends. We are called to love our enemies as well. When Paul wrote to the Roman church, he was writing to a group of believers who were a tiny minority in the city of Rome. They were oppressed and mistreated. Paul urged them to bless those who persecuted them instead of cursing them (Rom. 12:14). To bless others means praying for God's favor on them. We worship God when we honor those who do not honor us.

Our worship is put to the test when others mistreat us. When people hurt our families, friends, or us, our natural desire is to strike back. However, Paul challenged believers to respond differently. We are not to return evil for evil (Rom. 12:17; Matt. 5:43–48). We are called to respond with grace instead of reacting out of vengeance, behaving in such a way that even unbelievers around us can see the rightness of our actions. We are responsible to do everything in our power to live at peace with one another (Rom. 12:18). We don't stir up dissension; we seek peace. More than that, we refuse to take revenge (12:19). Our God is the only fair judge, and we should not take his responsibility into our hands.

Rather than matching evil with evil, we as believers should show kindness to those who have wronged us. In so doing, we will "heap burning coals on their heads" (12:20). Burning coals can be a symbol of judgment, but they can also be a symbol of repentance. When we respond to evil with good, our actions convict those who have wounded us and may lead them to repentance. Adding evil to evil doesn't eradicate evil; it multiplies evil. When we respond to evil with good, we reflect God's character and his goodness triumphs over evil.

Implications and Actions

Worship is our response to God's great mercy. Worship is not just something we do on Sunday; it is a way of life. We worship as God transforms our minds to conform us to Christ's image. We worship by using our gifts in humble service. We worship by committing ourselves to the hard work of relationships, devoting ourselves to acting in love and fighting for the unity of the body. We refuse to multiply evil by reacting out of our hurt. Instead, we bless when we are cursed and show kindness when we are mistreated, giving grace to all. We choose to live for God's glory instead of our own, and as we do, we worship.

ROGER WILLIAMS: FIRST BAPTIST IN AMERICA

Roger Williams, the founder of the colony of Rhode Island, also founded the first Baptist church in America. Williams was also one of our nation's first advocates for Native Americans. Williams used his gift for language to develop a close relationship with local tribes. He recognized that the Indians, not the king, were the true owners of the land and encouraged settlers to respect Indians' property rights. Williams understood that both the English and Indians were equally important and should be treated accordingly.

After Williams was banished from the Massachusetts Bay Colony for his religious beliefs, the Indians helped Williams survive. That relationship later helped save the colony. During the Pequot War of 1637, Massachusetts Bay leaders asked Williams to help make peace with the Native Americans. Even though some of these same leaders had banished him, Williams agreed. He risked his life by walking into a camp of 1,000 warriors to call for peace. His actions saved the lives of many settlers and may well have saved the colony from destruction.[1] His life is an example of forgiving others, serving others, and combating evil with good.

HOW TO APPLY THIS LESSON:

- Think of a group in your church whose service is often unrecognized. How could your class or small group show them honor?

- Pray for a difficult person in your life. How does God desire to bless that person? Pray for God's blessings on him or her and ask for the grace to respond in love.

- Look for points of application as you read Scripture. Is there a sin to confess, an action to take, a thought to change, or a prayer to pray? Take notes to keep a record of your spiritual transformation.

QUESTIONS

1. Sometimes when we read the Bible, we can be tempted to explain away or reinterpret challenging passages. How can we make sure that we are transformed by God's word instead of changing what it means to suit us?

2. What are your spiritual gifts? How are you using those gifts to pursue a lifestyle of worship?

3. In Romans 12, Paul stressed that worship isn't something we do in isolation; it should be part of our experience of Christian community. Why is corporate worship so important? Aside from Sunday morning worship, how does your church worship together?

4. Why is it so hard for us to love our enemies? What are some practical ways we can do good to those who hurt us without exposing ourselves to more harm?

5. What are some practical ways we can show "sincere love" for one another? What is one way your church does this well?

NOTES

1. Leon McBeth, *The Baptist Heritage* (Nashville: Broadman, 1987), 124–133; Lyn Garrity, "John Barry on Roger Williams and the Indians," *Smithsonian.com* (January 1, 2012) http://www.smithsonianmag.com/history/ john-m-barry-on-roger-williams-and-the-indians–9322792/?all. Accessed 3/27/2015.

FOCAL TEXT

Romans 13

BACKGROUND

Romans 13

LESSON 12

Civic Responsibility and Neighborly Love

MAIN IDEA

Gospel-centered living includes submitting to governmental authorities and loving our neighbors.

QUESTION TO EXPLORE

What are my responsibilities to the government and to my neighbors?

STUDY AIM

To recognize and embrace my responsibility to submit to governmental authorities and to express love to my neighbors

QUICK READ

Gospel-centered living requires me to submit to my government, love my neighbors, and be ready for Jesus' return.

Introduction

Today, Baptists make up the largest protestant denomination in the United States. Baptist churches thrive in all fifty states. We have Baptist hospitals, colleges, and private schools. Baptists have been on the Supreme Court and held the Oval Office. Baptists have enjoyed the benefits of a majority status, but they were not always so prominent.

During America's colonial period, Baptists were often a persecuted minority. Though the pilgrims who first settled New England came to the new world seeking religious freedom, they quickly established a state church and persecuted those who dared to dissent. They established the Congregational Church as the state church in most of New England, and colonial Baptists often clashed with the state over issues, like the taxes all citizens paid in support of the state church.

In 1652, a Baptist pastor named Reverend Obadiah Holmes was arrested and fined exorbitantly for preaching in a private home. Holmes refused to pay the fine and was whipped thirty times with a three-corded whip. Holmes continued preaching through the beating. Though he was severely injured, Holmes told the magistrates after the whipping, "You have struck me as with roses."[1]

Today, Baptists enjoy the benefits of our nation's religious liberty—a right we owe partially to early Baptists who fought for religious freedom. Though we enjoy freedom of religion, we can also see a downward shift in cultural attitudes toward Christianity. As other religions become more dominant and as more people consider themselves non-religious, we can envision a day when Christians become a minority once again. The letter to the Romans was written to people who made up a tiny fraction of the Roman population. They lacked influence and endured persecution. Yet, Paul called them to honor the government, love their neighbors, and be ready for Jesus' coming.

What would he say to us?

ROMANS 13

1 Everyone must submit himself to the governing authorities, for there is no authority except that which God has established. The authorities that exist have been established by God. 2 Consequently, he who rebels against the authority is rebelling against what God has instituted, and those who do so will bring judgment on themselves. 3 For rulers hold no terror for those who do right, but for those who do wrong. Do you want to be free from fear of the one in authority? Then do what is right and he will commend you. 4 For he is God's servant to do you good. But if you do wrong, be afraid, for he does not bear the sword for nothing. He is God's servant, an agent of wrath to bring punishment on the wrongdoer. 5 Therefore, it is necessary to submit to the authorities,

not only because of possible punishment but also because of conscience.

6 This is also why you pay taxes, for the authorities are God's servants, who give their full time to governing. 7 Give everyone what you owe him: If you owe taxes, pay taxes; if revenue, then revenue; if respect, then respect; if honor, then honor.

8 Let no debt remain outstanding, except the continuing debt to love one another, for he who loves his fellowman has fulfilled the law. 9 The commandments, "Do not commit adultery," "Do not murder," "Do not steal," "Do not covet," and whatever other commandment there may be, are summed up in this one rule: "Love your neighbor as yourself." 10 Love does no harm to its neighbor. Therefore love is the fulfillment of the law.

11 And do this, understanding the present time. The hour has come for you to wake up from your slumber, because our salvation is nearer now than when we first believed. 12 The night is nearly over; the day is almost here. So let us put aside the deeds of darkness and put on the armor of light. 13 Let us behave decently, as in the daytime, not in orgies and drunkenness, not in sexual immorality and debauchery, not in dissension and jealousy. 14 Rather, clothe yourselves with the Lord Jesus Christ, and do not think about how to gratify the desires of the sinful nature.

I Am Responsible for Honoring My Government (13:1–7)

Paul was not naïve about the Roman government's abuse of power. He knew Rome was responsible for Jesus' crucifixion. He had seen his Jewish countrymen expelled from the city. Yet, Paul still called the Roman church to honor the government. Why?

Paul understood that God established governing authorities to protect and provide for their citizens (13:1–2). This was not a new concept. Daniel recognized that all authority came from God (Daniel 4:17). Jesus said that God had granted Pilate's authority (John 19:11). In his sovereignty, God establishes governments and governing officials to exercise leadership and establish and maintain order. Our citizenship in the kingdom of God does not exempt us from our responsibilities as citizens of this world. We are called to submit to our government by acknowledging its authority over us and treating our governing officials with honor.

Since God has established government, those who rebel against governmental authority are rebelling against God (Rom. 13:2). In its role of rewarding good and punishing evil, governmental authority is God's agent for establishing and maintaining an ordered world. Government officials may deny God's existence and authority, but they still accomplish God's work as they administer justice.

If we deny that God has established governing authorities and reject their legitimate authority over us, we are rebelling against God's sovereignty and suffer the consequences of those actions. We should submit to government to avoid punishment, but we should also honor and submit to those who govern because God has granted them authority. Submission and respect toward government is an act of obedience and submission toward God.

Paul did not speak of Christians' attitudes toward government as mere principle. Honoring government must be reflected in our actions, including paying taxes. This may have been a contentious topic for the Roman believers. Rome's system of taxation was vulnerable to abuse, but Paul still called on Roman Christians to pay their taxes. He may have had in mind Jesus' instruction to "give to Caesar what is Caesar's and to God what is God's" (Mark 12:17). Government officials are God's servants, and it is our Christian responsibility to support them in their work by paying taxes.

Paul also knew an antagonistic relationship with the Roman government could hinder the spread of the gospel. Paul himself was a Roman citizen and did not hesitate to take advantage of the protection his citizenship provided (Acts 16:37–39; 22:25–29). Though this citizenship gave Paul some security, he also knew that Rome dealt harshly with any hint of rebellion. Open refusals to pay taxes would have brought Rome's iron boot down on the neck of the infant religion. Paul urged believers to pray for government officials and do what they could to be at peace with them (1 Timothy 2:1–2).

We should not take this passage as an endorsement of the Roman Empire's behavior, or as a blank check for governmental abuse. We are called to honor and respect our government; we are not asked to obey it blindly. We are ultimately responsible to God, and sometimes civil disobedience is necessary. However, such times are the exception and not the rule. If we disobey government, we must have a good reason for doing so, and we should be prepared to accept the consequences (Acts 4:19, 5:19; 1 Peter 2:13–14, 4:15–16).

I Am Responsible for Loving My Neighbors (13:8–10)

In these verses, Paul described believers' obligation to love as a "debt" we owe one another (13:8). Paul's instruction to owe no debt other than love does not forbid us from taking out a mortgage or car loan, although we should promptly repay what we owe. Rather, the emphasis is on the debt we all owe to one another: love. As Christ has loved us, so we should love one another (John 13:34). It is not a responsibility we should shirk. Our call to love one another is an urgent command.

Biblical love is an action that seeks the best for the other person. "Love does no harm to its neighbor" (Rom. 13:10).

Jesus said that the greatest commandments were to love God and love others (Mark 12:30-31). The Old Testament law gives instruction on how to love others. Love prompts us to care for the poor, to honor our parents, to pursue honesty, and to refrain from harming one another. Love compels us to seek justice and to treat others fairly. Love without a moral framework is only sentimentality. Morality without love is legalism and hypocrisy. Our love must be grounded in and measured by, the gospel. Jesus called us to holiness even as he gave his life for us (John 15:13). True love follows the Savior's example.

I Am Responsible for Preparing for My Savior's Coming (13:11–14)

Our responsibility to Christ undergirds and takes precedence over all other responsibilities. Honoring our government and loving our neighbors are only two facets of a gospel-centered life. Living a Christ-centered life also requires us to be alert, recognizing the times that we live in.

Imagine a soldier waking up in the dim light of dawn. He takes off his nightclothes and girds himself in his armor, ready for whatever the day might bring. Paul applied that imagery to the Christian life.

The time has come for believers to wake up from spiritual slumber because "our salvation"—the day of Christ's return—is nearer now than when we first believed. We do not know the timing of Christ's return, but we know that every day brings us closer to it. We must prepare ourselves by putting aside "the deeds of darkness" and putting on the "armor of light" (Rom. 13:12–13; Ephesians 6:10–17; Colossians 3:5–10).

Paul identified the deeds of darkness as carousing, drunkenness, sexual immorality, debauchery, dissension, and jealousy—all things that tend to happen at night. However, we should not consider this an exhaustive list. Sin—any sin—has no place in the Christian life. There is no such thing as "acceptable Christian sin." Gossip, lying, selfishness, greed, and an unforgiving attitude are also deeds of darkness. We need to repent of our sins, change our behavior, and cultivate obedience to Christ.

We can't put aside the deeds of darkness without putting on the armor of light. We can't stop lying unless we start telling the truth; nor can we stop being selfish without also putting others first. We clothe ourselves with Christ by developing Christ-like obedience and character. The Spirit makes us clean, but we participate in the process of spiritual transformation. Putting on the armor of light begins with the commitment that when a moment of decision comes, our choice is already made. We have chosen Jesus.

We should be so passionately consumed with following Christ that we don't look for escape clauses to obedience. We human beings tend to justify our actions. After all, going five miles an hour over the speed limit doesn't count as speeding; "little white lies" aren't so bad; it's not gossip, it's just venting. Putting on the armor of light requires us to stop making excuses for sin. The renewed mind does not look for ways to indulge in sin, no matter how pleasurable that sin may be. Instead, the renewed mind seeks to partner with God and his work in the world. Instead of indulging ourselves, we desire to please Christ. Like a soldier fully committed to duty, we should live fully committed to Christ as we eagerly anticipate his return.

Implications and Actions

Early Christians did not enjoy an easy relationship with the Roman government. Though the intensity of persecution varied, Christians were executed for refusing to worship the emperor. The emperors were corrupt, immoral, and insane. Yet, Paul recognized that God had ordained government and called Christians to honor those who wielded governmental authority. We honor government because we honor a Savior who did. Jesus respected Pilate's authority even as Pilate used that authority to condemn him to death.

Gospel-centered living doesn't just impact our attitudes toward government leaders who serve at a distance. It also impacts our relationships with those who live here with us in the messiness of life. We are called to love our neighbors with action, refraining from evil and seeking the benefit of those around us. Love is something we *show*. Jesus showed the world the Father's love, and we know he is returning quickly. That knowledge should spur us to be ready so that the Lord finds us obedient when he comes. Time is too short to waste on living for anything other than the Savior.

BAPTISTS AND THE SEPARATION OF CHURCH AND STATE

The first amendment to the United States Constitution establishes freedom of religion. It states,

> Congress shall make no law respecting an establishment of religion, or prohibiting the free exercise thereof; or abridging the freedom of speech, or of the press; or the right of the people peaceably to assemble, and to petition the Government for a redress of grievances.

Americans owe the existence of this amendment in part to the work of Baptists who lobbied legislators such as James Madison and Thomas Jefferson to guarantee religious liberty. In 1784, Virginia Baptists formed a General Committee to work for religious liberty. They wanted government to leave religion alone and attend to civil duties without meddling in religious affairs. Though they had some success in petitioning state legislatures, Baptists wanted a federal guarantee of religious liberty.

Virginia Baptists organized opposition to the new Constitution because it did not guarantee religious liberty. Baptists controlled enough votes that their opposition could have defeated the Constitution. James Madison met with Baptist leader John Leland in March of 1788. Leland withdrew his opposition to the Constitution in exchange for Madison's promise to introduce a set of constitutional amendments addressing Baptist concerns. The ten amendments Madison introduced became known as the Bill of Rights.[2]

CASE STUDY

You are enjoying dinner with a group of friends when the conversation turns political. Several members of the group not only disagree with a government official's position on a particular issue, but they also begin to speak of him in ways that make you uncomfortable. They call him names, malign his character, and speak of him in very disrespectful ways. You're not a fan of his politics, but the tone of the conversation is jarring. What do you do?

QUESTIONS

1. The Book of Romans was written to a Christian audience that was a minority living under the power of a pagan empire. What does Paul's call to honor governmental authority look like for us who live as citizens of a democracy?

2. How does our relationship with God shape our relationship to our government, even when we disagree with the actions of that government?

3. How is love the fulfillment of the law?

4. How should our belief in Christ's return shape our ethics and behavior?

5. In what specific ways can we shift from indulging our sinful nature to seeking out opportunities for obedience? How can this shift in mindset help us conquer temptation?

NOTES ————————————————————————

1. Leon McBeth, *The Baptist Heritage* (Nashville: Broadman, 1987), 140–141.

2. McBeth, 267–283.

FOCAL TEXT
Romans 14:1–21

BACKGROUND
Romans 14:1–21

LESSON 13

Personal Preference or the Pursuit of Harmony?

MAIN IDEA

Christians should seek harmony with other believers rather than insisting on their own preferences.

QUESTION TO EXPLORE

Does insistence on my preferences lead to disharmony in my church?

STUDY AIM

To pursue harmony with other believers instead of insisting on my preferences

QUICK READ

I am called to respect other believers and pursue harmony instead of judging those who do not conform to my personal preferences.

Introduction

Marriage requires the art of compromise. I found that to be true the first year of marriage. I learned from my mother how to cook a roast for Sunday dinner. She always made gravy and served it with potatoes and carrots cooked with the roast. After I got married, I carried on the tradition. I learned quickly that the Louisiana boy I married didn't eat potatoes with a roast. He wanted rice. I'd never heard of such a thing. Rice was a side dish to go with tacos or sweet and sour chicken. You don't mix it with peas and eat it with gravy.

Eating rice instead of potatoes was a small issue, but small disagreements left unresolved can mushroom into bigger conflicts. In our marriages, we have to learn not to do things "his way" or "her way," but to find "our way" together. Successful marriages require two people to work together in pursuit of harmony instead of insisting on having their own way.

Insisting on our way breeds conflict in churches, too. When we gather as the church, we bring together individuals from different backgrounds and walks of life. We all have personal opinions about the color of the carpet, the type of songs to sing, the ideal temperature of the sanctuary, and what kinds of activities should be offered for teens. While we cling tenaciously to the priesthood of the believer, we must guard against selfish attitudes that can damage fellowship in the body of Christ.

Demanding adherence to my point of view at the expense of others' needs leads to conflict. Our goal is not to have it our way. Our goal is God's way. In church life, as in marriage, we may need to compromise on non-essentials as we work together for harmony.

ROMANS 14:1–21

1 Accept him whose faith is weak, without passing judgment on disputable matters. 2 One man's faith allows him to eat everything, but another man, whose faith is weak, eats only vegetables. 3 The man who eats everything must not look down on him who does not, and the man who does not eat everything must not condemn the man who does, for God has accepted him. 4 Who are you to judge someone else's servant? To his own master he stands or falls. And he will stand, for the Lord is able to make him stand.

5 One man considers one day more sacred than another; another man considers every day alike. Each one should be fully convinced in his own mind. 6 He who regards one day as special, does so to the Lord. He who eats meat, eats to the Lord, for he gives thanks to God; and he who abstains, does so to the Lord and gives thanks to God. 7 For none of us lives to himself alone and none of us dies to himself alone. 8 If we live, we live to the Lord; and if we die, we die to the Lord. So, whether we live or die, we

belong to the Lord. [9] For this very reason, Christ died and returned to life so that he might be the Lord of both the dead and the living.

[10] You, then, why do you judge your brother? Or why do you look down on your brother? For we will all stand before God's judgment seat. [11] It is written:

"'As surely as I live,' says the Lord,
    'every knee will bow before me;
    every tongue will confess to God.'"

[12] So then, each of us will give an account of himself to God.

[13] Therefore let us stop passing judgment on one another. Instead, make up your mind not to put any stumbling block or obstacle in your brother's way. [14] As one who is in the Lord Jesus, I am fully convinced that no food is unclean in itself. But if anyone regards something as unclean, then for him it is unclean. [15] If your brother is distressed because of what you eat, you are no longer acting in love. Do not by your eating destroy your brother for whom Christ died. [16] Do not allow what you consider good to be spoken of as evil. [17] For the kingdom of God is not a matter of eating and drinking, but of righteousness, peace and joy in the Holy Spirit, [18] because anyone who serves Christ in this way is pleasing to God and approved by men.

[19] Let us therefore make every effort to do what leads to peace and to mutual edification. [20] Do not destroy the work of God for the sake of food. All food is clean, but it

is wrong for a man to eat anything that causes someone else to stumble. ²¹ It is better not to eat meat or drink wine or to do anything else that will cause your brother to fall.

Don't Quarrel Over Disputable Matters (14:1–9)

In Romans 14, Paul addressed two groups in the Roman church who insisted on their preferences—the "weak" and the "strong." Paul used these terms descriptively, not negatively or judgmentally. The "weak" abstained from eating meat and observed the celebration of special days. The "strong" felt free to eat meat and did not consider one day more important than another. Both groups were guilty of judging and trying to impose their preferences on the other.

The weak group was probably made up of Jewish believers who still felt compelled to observe the Old Testament law. Some Jews adopted vegetarian diets when it was difficult to procure meat prepared according to Jewish dietary standards. Furthermore, Jews often abstained from wine if they believed portions of it had been offered to pagan gods; Jewish law also called for the observance of several holy days. First century Jews often observed weekly days set aside for fasting and prayer in addition to the days required by the law.

This "weak" group in the Roman church did not believe their salvation depended on keeping these disciplines. Paul strongly condemned such teaching elsewhere (Galatians 3:1–6) and would most likely have challenged such a belief in Rome as well. It is more likely that the term "weak" represented a group of people who had accepted God's grace for salvation, but found it difficult to lay aside the ceremonial aspects of the Jewish faith. Since they were judging those who did not share their standards, the weak may have believed they were better Christians by adhering to these principles or that their preferences held a moral imperative and superiority.

This division was not a pure Jewish/Gentile rift, however. Paul himself was Jewish and certainly would have placed himself among the "strong," believing he had the freedom to eat as he liked. The strong were a group—most likely the majority—in the church who believed Christ had freed them from the constraints of the law. Some members of this "strong" group looked down on those who were more restrictive in their practices (the "weak"), perhaps feeling themselves spiritually superior to those who still felt compelled to follow Jewish dietary guidelines.

Early Christians recognized that some matters were moral imperatives regardless of the circumstances. In Romans 13, Paul dealt with topics that fell in this category, such as not taking revenge and being faithful to pay your taxes. However, early believers also recognized that some actions could be good or bad depending on the connotations for the person doing them. These would be thought of as "gray areas" in today's culture.

In Romans 14, Paul considered subjects such as eating meat and celebrating special days to be secondary to other, more important theological matters, and urged both groups to refrain from arguing over non-essential matters. Though Paul made clear his opinion, he also emphasized that these non-critical issues such as eating meat and observing special days are matters of conscience in which believers have freedom (14:14).

One who eats meat does not sin by doing so, and a person who eats only vegetables does not sin by abstaining from meat. Both groups are obeying their conscience before the Lord and should continue to do so. Like early believers, we should not waste energy by quarreling over secondary issues. On these issues, we should follow our consciences and avoid picking fights with others. We are free to follow our preferences, but we are not free to insist others agree with us.

Stop Judging One Another (14:7–12)

Believers still deal with differences of opinion in the church today. Some abstain from drinking alcohol; others say they believe it is fine to drink in moderation. Some refuse to shop on Black Friday or Thanksgiving evening;

others run to the stores to be the first in line. Some want the youth group to be a place of grace where all are welcome; others want the youth to learn discipline and to follow the rules. Some like to worship with choruses and drums, while others prefer hymns and an organ. We come with our set of preferences, and somehow our viewpoints tend to progress from "I like this better" to "my way is better" to "I am better than you." We see our opinions as extensions of ourselves and judge those who disagree with us accordingly. However, the grace God has extended to us should be reflected in our relationships with others. We should not judge one another over disputable matters.

We should not judge one another because our actions are based in reverence for Christ. Both those who exercise their freedom and those who draw tighter circles of constraint do so out of a desire to please the Lord. Christ's death and resurrection sealed him as Lord of all, and we are ultimately accountable to him (14:12). That does not mean we do not deal with sin or stop holding one another accountable, but when no biblical or moral principle has been violated, we need to step back and recognize that we are not the one in charge. It is the Spirit's role to convict, not ours. We need to trust the Spirit to do his work and not seek to compel others to share our view on issues where the Bible leaves us free to choose.

Likewise, we should not look down on those who follow a more restrictive faith than we do. If they sincerely love the Lord and desire to please him, then they will follow the Spirit's leadership accordingly. We do not have to conform to their practices, but we should not treat them contemptuously either. One day, we will all bow before God's throne and give an account of ourselves to him. Our accountability to God should impact how we treat one another.

Act in Love (14:13–21)

When extended family visits, I usually remind my children to be extra careful about picking up toys while their grandparents are here. We are simply being considerate— we don't want a toy to make Grandma trip and fall. We should have that same consideration for one another in the body of Christ. We should resolve not to put a stumbling block in the way of a brother or sister in Christ. We should not use our liberty in such a way that it puts pressure on someone else to violate his or her conscience and fall into sin. We should also avoid so offending another person with our freedom that we turn them away from the gospel.

For example, on mission trips we should take the effort to learn something about the host country's manners and dress codes. I may not feel compelled to cover my head in public, but I wouldn't want my lack of a head covering to turn someone away from hearing the gospel. Similarly, in parts of the country where the cultural belief is that "good

Christians" don't drink, it's prudent not to bring a bottle of wine to the church barbecue. Love constrains freedom. That doesn't mean I should give up playing cards if my neighbor thinks it's sinful; rather, if he comes to dinner I might pull out dominoes or a board game instead. Our freedom should not bring a brother or sister in Christ to spiritual ruin.

The Kingdom of God is about more than eating and drinking—or dancing, playing cards, or reading fiction novels. The Kingdom of God is about the righteousness, peace, and joy Christ has given us through the Holy Spirit. Dedicating ourselves to these things wins us favor both with God and with people. We need to make every effort to do what leads to peace and what builds one another up. Sometimes this means swallowing our pride—or our tongues. Sometimes it means laying aside our preferences for a moment so we don't offend or tempt a fellow believer. Our goal should always be the benefit of the body—not its destruction.

Implications and Actions

Our attitudes and actions in the body of Christ should always be motivated by love. We will not always agree with all people on all issues at all times. There are issues on which Scripture speaks clearly. We must adhere to God's commands on these matters, but there are other issues on which Christians can legitimately disagree. On these issues, we need to give one another grace.

When we encounter these disputable issues, we should listen and seek to understand one another instead of arguing and trying to convince others to adopt our convictions. We should neither look down on those who do not share our scruples nor hurl insults like "old-fashioned," or "narrow-minded." Instead, we should honor one another in love and respect each other's choices in non-essential matters. We are ultimately accountable to Christ, and he will hold us responsible for pursuing harmony.

COMMAND OR CONSCIENCE?

On some issues the Bible gives clear indications of right or wrong, sin or obedience. On some other issues, God allows us to follow our consciences. In Romans 14, Paul was not advocating an "anything goes" type of gospel. On the other hand, we need to choose our battles carefully. The following questions can help us discern which issues are disputable and which are essential.

- Does the Bible speak to this issue? Where Scripture speaks plainly, we must conform to it.

- What do other mature believers say about this issue? Seek the advice from faithful Christians who are committed to God's word.

- What good fruit is produced by it? Are people growing in Christ as a result? Are people harmed physically, emotionally, or spiritually by participating?

- Is it wrong for all people or just wrong for me? Is this wrong for me because of my personal issues, but may not be wrong for others?

CASE STUDY

Some of the youth approach you after the Sunday morning service. Their Sunday morning wardrobe is the same as the rest of the week—t-shirts, flip-flops, baggy shorts, and well-worn jeans. This morning, a few adults told them that they needed to dress up for church and "show some respect for God's house." Upset, the youth say if they can't be accepted as they are, they won't come back to church. What do you say to the youth? To the adults?

QUESTIONS:

1. What are some examples of issues that are essential to the faith? Issues that are disputable? How do we know which is which?

2. Why should we not judge one another over disputable issues?

3. What are some ways in which we can put a "stumbling block" or cause spiritual harm to another believer?

4. What are some practical ways in which love should constrain our freedom?

5. When church conflicts arise, how can we work for peace and the good of the body of Christ instead of insisting on our preferences?

Our Next New Study
(Available for use beginning December 2015)

JESUS: KING OR CONCIERGE?
A Study of the Gospel of Matthew

UNIT FOUR: THE PASSION OF THE KING

How to Order More Bible Study Materials

It's easy! Just fill in the following information. For additional Bible study materials available both in print and digital versions, see www.baptistwaypress.org, or get a complete order form by calling 1–866–249–1799 or e-mailing baptistway@texasbaptists.org.

Title of item	Price	Quantity	Cost
This Issue:			
Romans: A Gospel-Centered Worldview—Study Guide (BWP001202)	$4.25	_____	_____
Romans: A Gospel-Centered Worldview—Large Print Study Guide (BWP001203)	$4.50	_____	_____
Romans: A Gospel-Centered Worldview—Teaching Guide (BWP001204)	$4.95	_____	_____
Additional Issues Available:			
Created for Relationships—Study Guide (BWP001197)	$3.95	_____	_____
Created for Relationships—Large Print Study Guide (BWP001198)	$4.25	_____	_____
Created for Relationships—Teaching Guide (BWP001199)	$4.95	_____	_____
14 Habits of Highly Effective Disciples—Study Guide (BWP001177)	$3.95	_____	_____
14 Habits of Highly Effective Disciples—Large Print Study Guide (BWP001178)	$4.25	_____	_____
14 Habits of Highly Effective Disciples—Teaching Guide (BWP001179)	$4.95	_____	_____
Growing Together in Christ—Study Guide (BWP001036)	$3.25	_____	_____
Growing Together in Christ—Teaching Guide (BWP001038)	$3.75	_____	_____
Guidance for the Seasons of Life—Study Guide (BWP001157)	$3.95	_____	_____
Guidance for the Seasons of Life—Large Print Study Guide (BWP001158)	$4.25	_____	_____
Guidance for the Seasons of Life—Teaching Guide (BWP001159)	$4.95	_____	_____
Living Generously for Jesus' Sake—Study Guide (BWP001137)	$3.95	_____	_____
Living Generously for Jesus' Sake—Large Print Study Guide (BWP001138)	$4.25	_____	_____
Living Generously for Jesus' Sake—Teaching Guide (BWP001139)	$4.95	_____	_____
Living Faith in Daily Life—Study Guide (BWP001095)	$3.55	_____	_____
Living Faith in Daily Life—Large Print Study Guide (BWP001096)	$3.95	_____	_____
Living Faith in Daily Life—Teaching Guide (BWP001097)	$4.25	_____	_____
Participating in God's Mission—Study Guide (BWP001077)	$3.55	_____	_____
Participating in God's Mission—Large Print Study Guide (BWP001078)	$3.95	_____	_____
Participating in God's Mission—Teaching Guide (BWP001079)	$3.95	_____	_____
Profiles in Character—Study Guide (BWP001112)	$3.55	_____	_____
Profiles in Character—Large Print Study Guide (BWP001113)	$4.25	_____	_____
Profiles in Character—Teaching Guide (BWP001114)	$4.95	_____	_____
Genesis: People Relating to God—Study Guide (BWP001088)	$2.35	_____	_____
Genesis: People Relating to God—Large Print Study Guide (BWP001089)	$2.75	_____	_____
Genesis: People Relating to God—Teaching Guide (BWP001090)	$2.95	_____	_____
Exodus: Liberated for Life in Covenant with God—Study Guide (BWP001192)	$3.95	_____	_____
Exodus: Liberated for Life in Covenant with God—Large Print Study Guide (BWP001193)	$4.25	_____	_____
Exodus: Liberated for Life in Covenant with God—Teaching Guide (BWP001194)	$4.95	_____	_____
Ezra, Haggai, Zechariah, Nehemiah, Malachi—Study Guide (BWP001071)	$3.25	_____	_____
Ezra, Haggai, Zechariah, Nehemiah, Malachi—Large Print Study Guide (BWP001072)	$3.55	_____	_____
Ezra, Haggai, Zechariah, Nehemiah, Malachi—Teaching Guide (BWP001073)	$3.75	_____	_____
Psalms: Songs from the Heart of Faith—Study Guide (BWP001152)	$3.95	_____	_____
Psalms: Songs from the Heart of Faith—Large Print Study Guide (BWP001153)	$4.25	_____	_____
Psalms: Songs from the Heart of Faith—Teaching Guide (BWP001154)	$4.95	_____	_____
Jeremiah and Ezekiel: Prophets of Judgment and Hope—Study Guide (BWP001172)	$3.95	_____	_____
Jeremiah and Ezekiel: Prophets of Judgment and Hope—Large Print Study Guide (BWP001173)	$4.25	_____	_____
Jeremiah and Ezekiel: Prophets of Judgment and Hope—Teaching Guide (BWP001174)	$4.95	_____	_____
Amos, Hosea, Isaiah, Micah: Calling for Justice, Mercy, and Faithfulness—Study Guide (BWP001132)	$3.95	_____	_____
Amos, Hosea, Isaiah, Micah: Calling for Justice, Mercy, and Faithfulness—Large Print Study Guide (BWP001133)	$4.25	_____	_____
Amos, Hosea, Isaiah, Micah: Calling for Justice, Mercy, and Faithfulness—Teaching Guide (BWP001134)	$4.95	_____	_____
The Gospel of Matthew: A Primer for Discipleship—Study Guide (BWP001127)	$3.95	_____	_____
The Gospel of Matthew: A Primer for Discipleship—Large Print Study Guide (BWP001128)	$4.25	_____	_____
The Gospel of Matthew: A Primer for Discipleship—Teaching Guide (BWP001129)	$4.95	_____	_____
The Gospel of Mark: People Responding to Jesus—Study Guide (BWP001147)	$3.95	_____	_____
The Gospel of Mark: People Responding to Jesus—Large Print Study Guide (BWP001148)	$4.25	_____	_____
The Gospel of Mark: People Responding to Jesus—Teaching Guide (BWP001149)	$4.95	_____	_____
The Gospel of Luke: Jesus' Personal Touch—Study Guide (BWP001167)	$3.95	_____	_____
The Gospel of Luke: Jesus' Personal Touch—Large Print Study Guide (BWP001168)	$4.25	_____	_____
The Gospel of Luke: Jesus' Personal Touch—Teaching Guide (BWP001169)	$4.95	_____	_____
The Gospel of John: Believe in Jesus and Live!—Study Guide (BWP001187)	$3.95	_____	_____
The Gospel of John: Believe in Jesus and Live!—Large Print Study Guide (BWP001188)	$4.25	_____	_____
The Gospel of John: Believe in Jesus and Live!—Teaching Guide (BWP001189)	$4.95	_____	_____
The Book of Acts: Time to Act on Acts 1:8—Study Guide (BWP001142)	$3.95	_____	_____
The Book of Acts: Time to Act on Acts 1:8—Large Print Study Guide (BWP001143)	$4.25	_____	_____

Item	Price		
The Book of Acts: Time to Act on Acts 1:8—Teaching Guide (BWP001144)	$4.95	_____	_____
The Corinthian Letters—Study Guide (BWP001121)	$3.55	_____	_____
The Corinthian Letters—Large Print Study Guide (BWP001122)	$4.25	_____	_____
The Corinthian Letters—Teaching Guide (BWP001123)	$4.95	_____	_____
Galatians and 1&2 Thessalonians—Study Guide (BWP001080)	$3.55	_____	_____
Galatians and 1&2 Thessalonians—Large Print Study Guide (BWP001081)	$3.95	_____	_____
Galatians and 1&2 Thessalonians—Teaching Guide (BWP001082)	$3.95	_____	_____
Letters to the Ephesians and Timothy—Study Guide (BWP001182)	$3.95	_____	_____
Letters to the Ephesians and Timothy—Large Print Study Guide (BWP001183)	$4.25	_____	_____
Letters to the Ephesians and Timothy—Teaching Guide (BWP001184)	$4.95	_____	_____
Hebrews and the Letters of Peter—Study Guide (BWP001162)	$3.95	_____	_____
Hebrews and the Letters of Peter—Large Print Study Guide (BWP001163)	$4.25	_____	_____
Hebrews and the Letters of Peter—Teaching Guide (BWP001164)	$4.95	_____	_____
Letters of James and John—Study Guide (BWP001101)	$3.55	_____	_____
Letters of James and John—Large Print Study Guide (BWP001102)	$3.95	_____	_____
Letters of James and John—Teaching Guide (BWP001103)	$4.25	_____	_____

Coming for use beginning December 2015

Item	Price		
Matthew—Jesus: King or Concierge?—Study Guide (BWP001207)	$4.25	_____	_____
Matthew—Jesus: King or Concierge?—Large Print Study Guide (BWP001208)	$4.50	_____	_____
Matthew—Jesus: King or Concierge?—Teaching Guide (BWP001209)	$4.95	_____	_____

Cost
of items (Order value)   _____

Order Value	Shipping charge**	Order Value	Shipping charge**
$.01—$9.99	$6.50	$160.00—$199.99	$24.00
Standard (UPS/Mail) Shipping Charges*			
$20.00—$39.99	$9.50	$250.00—$299.99	$30.00
$40.00—$59.99	$10.50	$300.00—$349.99	$34.00
$60.00—$79.99	$11.50	$350.00—$399.99	$42.00
$80.00—$99.99	$12.50	$400.00—$499.99	$50.00
$100.00—$129.99	$15.00	$500.00—$599.99	$60.00
$130.00—$159.99	$20.00	$600.00—$799.99	$72.00**

Shipping charges
(see chart*)   _____

TOTAL   _____

*Please call 1-866-249-1799 if the exact amount is needed prior to ordering.

**For order values $800.00 and above, please call 1-866-249-1799 or check www.baptistwaypress.org

Please allow two weeks for standard delivery. For express shipping service: Call 1-866-249-1799 for information on additional charges.

YOUR NAME _____   PHONE _____

YOUR CHURCH _____   DATE ORDERED _____

SHIPPING ADDRESS _____

CITY _____   STATE _____   ZIP CODE _____

E-MAIL _____

MAIL this form with your check for the total amount to:
BAPTISTWAY PRESS, Baptist General Convention of Texas,
333 North Washington, Dallas, TX 75246-1798
(Make checks to "BaptistWay Press")

OR, **CALL** your order toll-free: 1-866-249-1799
(M-Fri 8:30 a.m.-5:00 p.m. central time).

OR, **E-MAIL** your order to: baptistway@texasbaptists.org.

OR, **ORDER ONLINE** at www.baptistwaypress.org.

We look forward to receiving your order! Thank you!